Note; The devil to [...]
but the Lord

Note: We will probably [...] respect
some way, every day.

Note: It doesn't matter what anyone says
about us. It only matter what God says about us.

BREAKING
BAD

Answering the Call
through Hell and High Water

BARRY MONDA

Thinking of a book or either a movie called
Prayer. Going into different prayers

www.xulonpress.com

Endorsements

"Barry's message is intimate, uplifting and very inspiring. As a writer myself, I must say that this book is a must read. It warms my heart to read "Breaking Bad." The events and stories in this book speak from the heart and true to life issues. The real life stories within stories will have you laughing and then they are so heartfelt they will have you crying. As I walked through the pages of "Breaking Bad" I found it to be insightful as it pertained to many of the experiences I have gone through in my life. It is powerful and I'm so grateful that I was able to be used by God to help Elder Barry get his life back on track and to become a success in life."

Bishop Donny Banks, Presiding Prelate

Victory Gospel Chapel, San Antonio, TX

"Barry Monda's, Breaking Bad, is the gripping story of one man's journey through addiction, recovery and transformation. Ultimately, it's the story of a loving God who has a plan for Barry and never gives up on him regardless of the struggles, the disappointments, the rebellion. This is also our story whether we recognize our addictions or not. Having known Barry and Melody during part of their journey before and after marriage, I can attest to the great work God has done and is doing in their lives. This book is an easy but convicting read."

Robert A. Martindale,

Lieutenant Colonel, US Army, Retired

President & CEO of SAMMinistries, Retired

Dedication

To my Lord Jesus Christ, for the power and mercy He has shown in my life, and most of all His grace without which I would be lost.

To my dad and mom: I thank my dad for all of the tough love over the years that eventually allowed me to learn through the consequences of my behavior. My mom, for her love toward me through it all. It is said and I believe that a mother's love toward her children is the closest to God's love. It's unconditional.

To my sisters, my son, Anthony, and the rest of my family who were sadly affected by all of my mess for a couple of decades. To my lovely wife, Melody, who knew me at my worst and witnessed the miraculous transformation, asked me to marry her and she's been putting up with me ever since.

To my Bishop, Dr. Donny Banks, who has been to me a spiritual dad, a friend, a counselor, advisor, teacher, and inspiration for my business and life. He took me in when no one else would, and he has been an example of following the Lord. He has shared his heart and shown me how to be a man after God's own heart.

To everyone at Parkway Baptist Church who prayed for me for over twenty years.

Acknowledgements

I thank my lovely wife, Melody. She is truly my Proverbs 31 woman who makes our house a home, whose children call her blessed, and who is worthy of praise and she adds to our income and has been an inspiration and a great help in the writing of this book.

Thank you to my son, Anthony, for allowing me to witness your miraculous transformation through our letters, phone conversations, visits and all of your Poems from Prison.

Thank you to my Bishop, Dr. Donny Banks, who imparted into me God's Word from his heart to my heart that enabled me to write this book.

Table of Contents

Born with a Disease Called Sin

He takes me

He breaks me

He blesses me

He gives me

He saved me

He forgave me

He changed me

He rearranged me

He put me on top and everything under my feet.

He made me the head and not the tail

Above only and not beneath

Joint heir

Covered by His blood

The lender and not the borrower, a son. . .

I can decree and declare.

I can call those things which are not as though they were:

I am rich. I am strong.

I am a millionaire for the furthering of the kingdom of God.

By faith I am a published author of a bestseller
that points to Jesus Christ,
the author and finisher of my faith the Hope of Glory.
He planted me right here right now for His purpose,
His pleasure and for my good.

One of the biggest mistakes you or I can make is to transplant ourselves in the soil of the world's ways instead of staying planted in the soil of His mercy being watered by the river of His Spirit.

We must stay planted by faith; only then will we see the glory of God.

Introduction

Beat Down

Deep, dark secrets abound, and there are so many.
Some I'll tell. Some I won't.

God had given me extraordinary coordination, chosen me to shoot the winning shot at the buzzer, run the winning touchdown in the final seconds, hit the home run with two strikes against me, make the unbelievable catch at third base, and date the prettiest cheerleader. So how did I become a crackhead?

I always dreamed of becoming a famous football, basketball, or baseball player, but never a player in the life of addiction. There are so many times I should've been found dead, ended up in prison, or infected with AIDS.

I can remember one time "jonesing" for another fix. I drove on down to the projects where it was like a drive-through for a drug score. You pull up and give them your money, get the dope, and drive off. Cars were parked on both sides of the street. There was a narrow passageway with room enough for one car. While stopped and doing my dope deal, all I had was a couple of dollars. So, I folded them up to where you couldn't see the numbers on the bills and asked for a large amount of dope. I made the transaction and began my getaway. To my surprise, a car was coming in the other direction. I tried to squeeze by, but my bumper got hung up on a parked car's bumper. Desperately trying to go backwards and forwards, spinning my tires, I was stuck.

About that time, the dope dealer realized that I had pulled a scam, a fast one. The car that I was stuck against and doing damage to in my efforts to escape was his! The next thing I knew there were people climbing and jumping on top of my car, busting out my windows, pulling on my door handles, and rocking the car back and forth. The devil had released the "Cracken." I remember it like it was yesterday. Seeing my only way out, I slid to the backseat. The only place I might get out safely was the back door. Against the parked car, there was just enough room to squeeze out, so I took a deep breath, popped the lock, and made a run for it.

Back in high school, I was second-leading rusher in the football league, but after going days without sleep on a crack binge, I didn't get very far. Running for my life, I looked behind me and I swear it looked like the Dallas Cowboys were chasing me—some big, some tall, some short, some fat, some skinny like me, dope dealers, and crack heads—all in a desperate pursuit with a vengeance. I ran until I couldn't run anymore. Finally, I fell to the ground and that's when they began to kick me and beat me with tree branches they used as clubs.

The crack heads went through my pockets dodging the kicks and the sticks meant for me. All I can remember saying over and over was, "I'll make it right. Let me make it right."

The beating seemed like it took forever and a day. When they finally stopped, they left me with broken ribs, a broken nose, a broken tooth, and with no strength left to stand. I had no crack, no car, and no dignity. Like a stray dog that had been hit and mangled by a car, I somehow crawled three blocks up the steps of somebody's front porch and knocked, crawled back down and collapsed in their front yard.

Aggravated when they came to the door because it was three in the morning, they yelled out, "WHAT?!"

I said weakly, "Please, call an ambulance."

They slammed the door, and I just laid there thinking it was the end, exhausted, and wondering what to do next.

A couple of minutes later, the front door opened back up and a nicer, more concerned voice spoke saying, "The ambulance is on the way."

I was very fragile, everything hurt; I could barely breathe.

No Mercy at the Hospital

When I arrived at the hospital, the first thing they did was a blood test. They told me that I should be dead because of the amount of cocaine that was in my system. They were not happy about it and showed great disgust to the point they did not even want to touch me.

They knew I'd been at this a long time. No one needed to take blood to know that I was a crack head. I looked the part—all skin and bones.

The attendants were ruthless and showed absolutely no compassion. They were mean and unsympathetic. I was in so much pain that they could not lay me down to take x-rays. They took them with me standing up. If I made any kind of sound or cried out that I was in pain, they would tell me to shut up and stop crying. They continued the verbal abuse and were physically rough with me during their treatment of my injuries. Everything they did to me caused more pain. It got so intense that my body shut down, and I passed out.

As I came to, they were picking me up off the floor. They acted frustrated with me like I was wasting their time and showed me no mercy. Then they sent me out into the emergency waiting room and told me, "You can't stay here."

At this point in my life, I had no friends and no family because I had pushed them all beyond their limits and nobody wanted me around. I don't know why, but for some reason I asked if I could use the phone. Surprisingly, they let me. I think they would have done anything to get me out of there. I called my parents.

Surprised by Mercy

I remember my mom answering the phone. I told her that I had been beaten up and was at the hospital. I asked if they would come and get me. Next thing I knew, I was talking to my dad who at our last run-in, had chased me off with a big stick of his own when I showed up at their house uninvited. This time, however, I witnessed God's great mercy.

My dad said to me, "I'm on my way."

My Dad and Me

I mostly slept for the next two weeks, exhausted from the beating and running hard for the devil. My parents waited on me hand and foot. My ribs were broken so I couldn't do anything but lay there. If I coughed or sneezed or moved even the slightest bit, it was like being stabbed with an ice pick with a direct hit to my rib cage. It was a long, painful road to recovery. I believe it was about six months before I completely recovered.

That's how I ended up in San Antonio, Texas.

The Shepherd and the Lamb

Roy Gustafson, who has led many parties to Israel, tells in his book, "In His Hand," that on one of his visits, on the road down from Jerusalem through the Judean wilderness to Jericho, they met a shepherd carrying one of his sheep that had a splint and a bandage on its leg.

Their guide, who'd lived nearly fifty years in that area, said, "The shepherd broke that sheep's leg himself."

It was true! It was explained to us that this was a sheep that was always wandering off, and in the process had been leading other sheep astray. Membership in the flock carries certain responsibilities, and much as the shepherd feels a real affection for his animals, discipline is the only thing that will keep them together. They must be kept together for their well-being and their safety.

So, to cure this sheep of its self-willed ways, the shepherd had broken its leg, and then hand fed and carried it until the bone was mended and (hopefully) its waywardness as well.[1]

This is the process the loving Shepherd took me through. This poem by an unknown author describes this process.

---

[1]   Roy Gustafson, "In His Hand," p.46

The Shepherd and the Lamb

The Shepherd loved His little lamb,
And gave it His tender care
And followed it with His loving eyes
As it wandered here and there.

And as He sat by His grazing flock
Who so meekly His voice obeyed,
He pondered sadly His little lamb
As again it strayed.

The little lamb had a loving heart,
And adored His Shepherd, true,
But would turn aside and seek his own way
As lambs so often do.

With His gentle voice the Shepherd called,
To His loved and straying lamb,
"Come back, little one, for you are not safe
Unless you are where I am."

But still the lamb would soon forget
And unthinkingly wander away,

And not really noticing what he did,
From the Shepherd's side would stray.

Until one day, the Shepherd kind
Took His rod in His gentle hand,
And what He then did seemed so cruel
That the lamb could not understand.

For with one sharp and well-aimed blow
Down the rod so swiftly came
That it broke the leg of the little lamb
And left it crippled, and lame.

Then the little lamb, with a cry of pain,
Fell down upon his knees,
And looked up at his Shepherd, as though to say,
"Won't You explain this, please?"

Then he saw the love in the Shepherd's eyes
As the tears ran down His face,
As He tenderly set the broken bone,
And bound it back in its place.

Now he was utterly helpless,
He could not even stand!

He must trust himself completely
To his Shepherds loving hand.

Then day by day, 'till the lamb was healed
From the flock he was kept apart,
And carried about in the Shepherd's arms
And cradled near to His heart.

And the Shepherd would whisper gentle words
Into his now listening ear,
Thus he heard sweet words of love
That the other sheep could not hear.

He felt the warmth of the Shepherd's arms.
And the beat of His faithful heart,
Until it came a blessing to seem,
By his weakness to be set apart.

Every need of the little lamb
By his Shepherd so fully was met
That through his brokenness he learned
What he never again would forget.

And as the broken bone was healed,
And once more became whole and strong,

Wherever the Shepherd's path would lead,
The lamb would follow along.

Thus at the Shepherd's side he walked
So closely, day by day,
For once a lamb has a broken leg
It will never again go astray.

For the cords of love had bound it so
In its hour of weakness and need,
That it had no desire to wander away,
When once again it was freed.

Could it be you are broken today,
And you cannot understand
The painful blow of the Shepherd's rod
Nor believe it came from His Hand?

He only seeks, by this painful thing,
For a time to call you apart,
To cradle you close in His loving arms,
And draw you near to His heart.

So look up into your Shepherd's eyes,
And earnestly seek His face,

And prove in the hour of your weakness and need
The sufficiency of His grace.

For as you are borne in His loving arms,
And carried there, day by day,
He will bind you so close with the cords of His love
That never again will you stray!

Do Not Despise the Chastening of the Lord

Behold, happy is the man whom God corrects; therefore, do not despise the chastening of the Almighty. For He bruises, but He binds up; He wounds, but His hands make whole. (Job 5:17-18 NKJV)

Jesus is the Good Shepherd. He loves us too much to leave us in our current condition. Rather than allow us to continue on our path of destruction, He will do whatever is needed to bring about our course correction, even to the point of disciplining us. The good news is, though we are bruised and wounded in these storms of correction, He binds up those wounds and makes us whole.

"My son, do not make light of the discipline of the Lord,
And do not lose heart and give up when you are corrected by Him;

For the Lord disciplines and corrects those whom He loves,

And He punishes every son whom He receives and welcomes [to His heart]."

(Hebrews 12:5-6 AMP)

Ask Yourself. . .

- *What bad behaviors, feelings, thoughts, and attitudes need to be broken by the Shepherd in my life?*
- *Who can I turn to right now who will tell me the truth I need to hear and show me God's mercy?*
- *Am I resisting the Shepherd's chastening and correction?*
- *Am I willing to surrender my pride to receive His mercy?*
- *Am I now willing to be trained by the disciplining of the Lord?*

Poems from Prison

With Jesus on my side,
It's impossible to lose.

Cry out for Him to save,
Never will He refuse!

It's my whole purpose,
To let His light Shine,

So others might see
And no longer walk blind.

Times running out,
This is plain as can be,

I illuminate His light
So everyone can see!

By Anthony Monda

Chapter 1

Arguing, Fussing, and Fighting

My dad is full-blooded Italian. My mom is Irish Indian. Arguing, fussing, and fighting with an occasional food fight were the norm in our house. One thing for sure, my household was never boring. In their early twenties with three kids, it was a recipe for disaster. My parents were always in hot pursuit of who did it and what for. As far as I knew at the time, we were just as dysfunctional as any other family.

As I look back now at all our adventures, I realize how even in the midst of all the fussing, fighting, and disgruntled confusion, God was there watching over and protecting us.

Dad and Mom

Early on, we discovered how each of us was gifted. Dina played the piano by ear and sang like a bird. I had extraordinary coordination which made me well qualified to play sports. At first, it seemed that Micca's "gift" was that she was spoiled rotten because she was the baby. Today, Micca is a published author with Proverbs 31 Ministries, travels the United States speaking to churches about Jesus and sharing words of healing, hope, and freedom through her life experiences. So, I guess you could say she had two gifts.

Monda kids: Barry, Micca, Dina

As I look back, I see God's hand on my life starting at a very young age. When I was around five years old, I was balancing myself on top of a rubber ball keeping my balance with one hand on the stereo and the other holding a ruler.

My mother, who was sitting on the couch, looked up and said, "You better stop that before you fall and ram that ruler down your throat."

Those words had barely come out of her mouth when I lost my balance, fell forward, and rammed that ruler down my throat. I don't really remember any pain, though. Maybe I was in shock. I do remember my mother frantically stuffing a wash cloth in my mouth that instantly turned red as she tried to stop the flow of blood. The last thing I remember before they put me out was being in the hospital with my arms, legs, and body strapped down on top of a table. After they had stitched me up, I was offered some ice cream. I always wondered how they got all those stitches way back there in my throat, though.

As a small child, my eardrums would burst. After the second or third time this happened and nothing was done about it going to our regular doctor, my parents decided to get a second opinion. It was a good thing they did because this new doctor said if my eardrums had burst one more time I could have lost my hearing. The problem was actually being caused by my adenoids. Once they were removed I was fine. However, I would like to blame my eardrums bursting for my trouble understanding my teachers at school. It was like the Charlie Brown cartoon when the adults spoke. All I heard was, "Wah, wah, wah." It wasn't my eardrums. It was because I thought I was dumb. I automatically thought I couldn't understand. Earl Nightingale says in his book, *The Strangest Secret*, "you become what you think about."

Going off the Deep End

Jumping off the Deep End

When I was seven years old, I began swimming lessons. After my first lesson, I decided I was ready for the deep end. Of course, I didn't come to this conclusion all by myself. My friend with the gift of gab and the power to persuade talked me into it. According to him, he was going to be with me all the way. Standing at the edge of the pool where the deep and shallow water meet, we were to jump in together on the count of three and then swim across the deep end of the pool.

The only problem was my buddy jumped toward the shallow end. I saw him out of the corner of my eye, and in that split second before

I hit the deep water, I lost all faith in my ability to swim. Like dead weight, I went straight to the bottom. In desperation, I planted my feet and with bended knees, I pushed off as hard as I could from the bottom of the pool and made it to the top gasping for air. Then I dropped back down to the pool bottom. I did this over and over and over again, until with no strength left, I was finally rescued.

Growing up in a world of trouble, sometimes we forget what we've already learned. I probably could have at least turned around and swam back to the side of the pool I had just jumped off of. Instead, I forgot all that I had learned and allowed fear to keep me bouncing up and down, using up all my strength until I was rescued. We do the same thing in our Christian walk. We forget what we have learned from God's Word and allow fear to paralyze us. Faith energizes, but fear keeps us from moving forward and steals our freedom.

The fear of man brings a snare, but whoever trusts in the LORD shall be safe. (Proverbs 29:25 NKJV)

An acronym for fear is:
False
Evidence
Appearing
Real

However, we can't pray fear away, we have got to confront it. We cannot let fear of what could happen paralyze us so nothing happens. Stagnation eventually brings death. Don't forget everything you've learned and sink to the bottom of the pool in fear. Face that fear, whatever it is, and you will rise to the top victorious. Everything you want is on the other side of your fear. The only way to fight fear is with faith. You must have faith in the Good Shepherd.

The LORD is my shepherd;
I shall not want.
He makes me to lie down in green pastures;
He leads me beside the still waters.
He restores my soul;
He leads me in the paths of righteousness
For His name's sake.

Yea, though I walk through the valley of the shadow of death,
I will fear no evil;
For You are with me;
Your rod and Your staff, they comfort me.

You prepare a table before me in the presence of my enemies;
You anoint my head with oil;
My cup runs over.
Surely goodness and mercy shall follow me
All the days of my life;
And I will dwell in the house of the LORD
Forever.

(Psalm 23 NKJV)

Take a step out of your comfort zone, step into faith in God, and go to the other side of the pool. Remember what you have learned about the Good Shepherd and embrace the freedom to be who God has called you to be. It is time to take that step of faith or you will never reach the other side. Step out of the boat in faith and begin to walk toward Jesus knowing He will not let you drown. Even though Peter momentarily took his eyes off of Jesus after he took that step of faith out of the boat, when the storm threatened to overtake him, Jesus stretched out His hand and pulled him to safety (Matthew 14:29-31). Peter put action to his faith, and though he stumbled, his faith was rewarded by Jesus.

What is the benefit, my fellow believers, if someone claims to have faith but has no [good] works [as evidence]? Can that [kind of] faith save him? [No, a mere claim of faith is not sufficient—genuine faith produces good works.] (James 2:14 AMP)

Cowboys and Indians

For where jealousy and selfish ambitions exist there will be disorder and every evil practice. (James 3:16)

My neighbor wanted to play cowboys and Indians. I was chosen to be the Indian.

After tying me up with rope to an old rusty swing set, he ran several yards away then yelled, "Now try and get away, Injun."

As I struggled vigorously to try and get away, I ended up shaking the swing set back and forth. Suddenly, disturbed by the shaking, wasps began to fly out from inside the top pipe. In full attack mode, they started stinging me all over my body. I wished I had not agreed to let my "friend" tie me up making it impossible for me to defend myself or escape the attack.

Another time we were out in his backyard making mushroom clouds. We would fill up coffee cans with dirt, throw them up in the air, and when they hit the ground they would explode into giant mushroom clouds of dust. Once the coffee cans were full of dirt, they were pretty heavy. We were taking turns filling them and throwing them up in the air as fast as we could.

Suddenly, my "friend" broke the rules and tossed his coffee can full of dirt up over my head. I didn't know which way to run and dared not look up. In my moment of hesitation, the coffee can full of dirt came down right on top of my head. That incident earned me five stitches. I was the youngest and the most gullible of the neighborhood kids, if you haven't figured that out by now.

I can remember getting a new bicycle for my birthday. One of my neighborhood friends said we ought to go riding and try out my new bike. We were riding side-by-side when I noticed tears coming down from his eyes. At the time I thought it was just the wind, but after what happened next, I am not sure. Without warning, he lifted his foot off the pedal and swerved his bike over toward me, rammed his pedal into the spokes of my front wheel. Of course, I crashed and burned, and my brand new bike was ruined. I now think those were tears of envy and jealousy in my "friend's" eyes.

As Christians we should not be too gullible. We are not called to be doormats letting everyone wipe their feet on us. In Matthew 10:16, when He sent His disciples out among the people to minister in His name, Jesus told them, "I am sending you out like sheep with wolves all around you. Be wise like snakes and gentle like doves" (NLT). As Christians, we may face hostility from those who claim to be our friends, but like the disciples, we are not to be sheep-like in our attitude. We are to be sensible and prudent and not to be gullible. Neither are we to be conniving. We must find a balance between wisdom and vulnerability to accomplish God's work.

My Neighborhood Gang Barry is third from the right.

Bare-footing for the Checkered Flag

One of my friends had little pedal cars that we would race on his back patio. You guessed it, with my innate physical abilities I always won. My car was even handicapped because one of the rubber pedals was missing, though the sharp little metal tie clip used to hold on the rubber pedal was still in place. My playmate insisted I race him barefoot

25

to make it a more even match. I was one of those kids who never went barefoot. I had such tender feet that I even slept with my socks on. However, being competitive I took on the challenge. Though I knew that I had to be careful pedaling barefoot because of the sharp, rusty metal tie, I took off my shoes and socks and off to the races we went. I was in the lead like always until my foot slipped right across that sharp metal tie and sliced my foot wide open. The race was over as I ran on my heel all the way home in painful regret as I received more stitches.

As a gullible child and most of my adulthood, I continually put myself in the same position and always got hurt. It reminds me of the parable of the hole.

I walked down the street.

There is a deep hole in the sidewalk.

I fall in. I am lost. I am helpless.

It isn't my fault.

It takes forever to find my way out.

I walked down the same street.

There is a deep hole in the side walk.

I pretend I don't see it.

I'll fall in again.

I can't believe I'm in the same place, but it's still not my fault.

It's still takes a long time getting out.

I walked down the street there is a deep hole in the sidewalk.

I see it is there. But I still fall in.

It's a habit. My eyes are open. I know where I am.

It is my fault.

I get out immediately.

I walked down the same street,

there is a deep hole in the side walk.

I walked around it.

I walked down a different street.

-Portia Nelson

In his book, *The Purpose Driven Life*, Rick Warren talks about defeating temptation. If you're losing the battle against a persistent bad habit, an addiction, or a temptation, and you're stuck in a repeating cycle of good intention/failure/guilt, you will not get better on your own; you need help. Some temptations are only overcome with the help of a partner who prays for you, encourages you, and holds you accountable. God's plan for your growth and freedom includes other Christians. Authentic, honest fellowship is the antidote to your lonely struggle against those sins that won't budge. God says it is the only way you're going to break free. Confess your sins to each other and pray for each other so that you may be healed (James 5:16). God's solution is plain: Don't repress it, confess it. Don't conceal it, reveal it. Revealing what you're feeling is the beginning of healing.[2]

---

[2]   *The Purpose Driven Life*, Rick Warren, p. 212

Forgotten

I was probably nine or ten years old when I began to play on the basketball team. The coach's son was the best player on the team. Looking through his dad's eyes, I was his son's only real competition. I was the only one who threatened his son's position. Of course, there was plenty of room for both of us to play, so I didn't see myself as a threat. I just wanted to have fun. However, even then I could see that my God given ability had an effect on others especially adults if their children were involved.

The coach would always pick me up and drive me to the games. Excitedly anticipating the upcoming game, I got dressed in my basketball uniform one afternoon, jumped on the couch facing the picture window, and waited impatiently for my ride to arrive. Mind you there were no cell phones back then. When it got dark and they still hadn't come for me, I remember the terrible feeling of being forgotten. With every headlight of every car that approached, hope swelled up inside of me only to be let down over and over and over again. My mom says I looked out the window hoping they would come for over two hours. Their excuse was they forgot about me.

Basketball Team, Barry bottom row, second from the right

You can live several days without food, about three days without water, but not one second without hope. Today Jesus is my hope.

Jesus Is My Hope

And not only that, but we also glory in tribulations, knowing that tribulation produces perseverance; and perseverance, character; and character, hope. Now hope does not disappoint, because the love of God has been poured out in our hearts by the Holy Spirit who was given to us. (Romans 5:3-6 NKJV)

Paul tells us that we have hope in the future, but we will experience difficulties that help us grow in the present. We rejoice in the suffering, not because we like pain or deny its tragedy, but because we know God is using life's difficulties to build our character. The problems that we run into will develop our patience which in turn will strengthen our character, deepen our trust in God, and give us greater confidence about the future. We will probably find our patience tested in some way every day. We need to thank God for those opportunities to grow and deal with them in His strength.

> **You can live several days without food, about three days without water, but not one second without hope. Today Jesus is my hope.**

However, we also need to be aware of the fact that we live in a world of trouble and bad things happen to good people. The enemy has been waging war against God and His kingdom since the beginning. First with God in heaven, (Revelation 12:7), then with Jesus at the cross (John 13:27), and now with us (1 Peter 5:8). The enemy has a plot, a ploy, and a plan to take us out early in life so we do not fulfill our God given purpose in life.

In John 10:10, Jesus warned, "The thief comes not, but for to steal, and to kill, and to destroy: I am come that they might have life, and that they might have it more abundantly" (KJV). In contrast to the thief who takes, Jesus gives. The life He gives now is abundantly richer and fuller. It is eternal, yet it begins immediately when we choose Him as our Lord and Savior. Life in Him is life on a higher plane because of His overflowing forgiveness, love, and guidance.[3]

Stolen Identity

The devil stole my identity early on. I still remember those words ringing in my ear, "He's just shy." My parents were explaining my demeanor. The truth is I had super-duper low self-esteem. I was afraid and ashamed and I didn't know why. When I turned eight, I began playing organized sports. The uniforms made me feel safe, especially football. I was covered from head to toe, helmet to cleats. I was better at basketball than any other sport, but I was never able to shine because I allowed my low self-esteem to get in the way. In the '70s, basketball uniforms were a skin tight tank top and short shorts. Wearing them made me feel naked and exposed. In combination with bleachers full of people hugging the court, I was terrified. I never seemed to find the balance between this low self-esteem and my extraordinary God given talent. Later in my early thirties at a spiritual growth center in Kentucky, I began to play basketball just about every day and did finally begin to shine.

---

[3]   Application Study Bible K JV Commentary

Naked and Ashamed

The definition of the word shy is uncomfortable with others, timid, easily frightened, unwilling to put trust and confidence in others. Later, I learned that being shy in certain situations was because at some point during my life I was extroverted, active, and social and it was met with a negative response, probably on more than one occasion. So, growing up my focus was on what's wrong with me, *I just couldn't get passed it.* Negative thinking is the root of low self-esteem. We tell ourselves we don't deserve to be happy or we are not good enough. With no eye contact, no words and no understanding when it came to school, I labeled myself deaf and dumb at an early age.

For as he thinks in his heart, so is he. (Proverbs 23:7)

As Christians, we learn that it doesn't matter what anybody says about us. It only matters what God says about us. He says we are beautifully and wonderfully made. He knitted us together in our mother's womb to be exactly who He wanted us to be (author paraphrase of Psalm 139:13-16).

So, in life we will be criticized, ostracized, and shunned. Aristotle says, "To avoid criticism say nothing, do nothing, be nothing." The more you do the more someone will have something negative to say about it. Don't let negative people steal your identity and keep you from living your dream. Erase the lie and replace it with the truth. Replace it with what God says about you. Study His word and allow God's love and His truth to make you free (John 8:32).

Jesus is the truth that makes us free. He is the source of truth, the perfect standard of what is right. He frees us from the consequences of sin, from self-deception, and from deception by Satan. He shows us clearly the way to eternal life with God. Thus, Jesus does not give us freedom to do what we want, but freedom to follow God. As we seek to serve God, Jesus' perfect truth frees us to be all that God meant us to be.[4]

---

[4] Application Study Bible KJ V Commentary

Teen Challenge Cape Girardeau, Missouri
Supernatural Manifestation of God's Presence

However, it wasn't until a few years later when I was in a church service at Teen Challenge Cape Girardeau that I began to understand who I really was in God. I was a thirty-three-year-old addict attempting to get my life back. The atmosphere was thick with God's presence and the weight of His glory forced me to the ground when tongues and interpretation came forth. I began to cry out loud uncontrollably. It was a good cry, a wonderful cry, a refreshing cry, a love story cry.

For the first time I was able to see clearly who I was and what I was compared to God. I was so small, so tiny, so minute, so dirty, and so filthy, but so loved. The only way I can explain it is the Bible says that our righteousness is dirty, filthy rags compared to God's righteousness (Isaiah 64:6). Crying was something I never did, especially out loud. Early in my childhood I had gotten good at holding back my emotions. I had learned not to let anyone see what I was feeling. God wasn't finished with me yet, though.

Later, when I was forty-four years old attending a Friday night Bible study at Victory Gospel Chapel, the teacher came in and began by saying there was a sweet spirit in the room. Of course, it was God. He went on to declare that there was somebody in the room that had made up their mind and was ready to make a decision to follow Christ. I was thinking to myself, *That's me!* Then Boom! God's presence hit me like a ton of bricks and once again I began to cry like a baby. God's strong presence had a voice saying, "Yes, it's you."

In another class God had put it upon the teacher's heart to pray eight blessings over each student: Mentally, spiritually, socially, sexually, intellectually, financially, materially, and physically. I can remember we all lined up to receive the blessings of God. I was somewhere in the middle of the line. When it was my turn, he anointed my head with oil and began to pray. The anointing was so strong that the people that went before me got back in line. As my faith kicked in, the tears began to flow uncontrollably. I knew God was doing something special. Somehow I knew without a shadow of doubt that all of these blessings were going to come true in my life, especially intellectually which was the one I felt I needed the most.

God uses people to bless us, to speak into our lives, and we should never take it for granted. That is why God tells us not to forsake the assembling of the saints as some do, because it will affect our faith. Everything in God is by faith. Without faith it is impossible to please God (Hebrews 11:6). The just shall live by faith (Romans 1:17). We need others that have walked the path before us to lead and guide us.

Ask Yourself. . .

- *Do I feel I was gullible as a child? Did other children take advantage of me?*
- *How susceptible to peer pressure was I as a child? Did others dare me to do things that were dangerous?*

- *Were there children or adults who put labels on me that I believed were true?*
- *Will you allow God's truth to set you free from those labels so you can become all that God has called and designed you to be?*

Poems from Prison

Have you ever been the son of a doped up father?
I have, I've been left home alone for days with no one to bother.
Do you know what it feels like to be moved from home to home, school to school?
I do, I've been chewed up and spit out so many times it ain't even cool,
Then my father got up off the ground, and with God's help,
he turned his life around.
In everything he did he worshipped the Lord,
So God gave him back everything the devil stole and more.

- Anthony Monda

Chapter 2

God Was There

eneration and have been since Adam and Eve. They can be out of control anger, spousal abuse, child abuse, verbal and physical abuse, incest, molestation, poverty, divorce, or alcoholism, just to name a few. To break these generational curses, we have to denounce them and come into agreement with every word that proceeds out of the mouth of God.

Generational Curse: Face It, Trace It, Erase It, and Replace It.

Face it, we live in a fallen world where bad things happen to good people. The word fallen is used in the Bible to describe someone or something spiritually and morally degraded.

For all have sinned and fall short of the glory of God. (Romans 3:23)

Trace it back to the devil, who from the beginning has come to steal our identities, kill our dreams, and destroy our destinies.

The thief comes only to steal and kill and destroy. I came that they may have life and have it abundantly. (John 10:10)

Erase it and replace it, by replacing the lie with the truth. Replace it with what God says and thinks about you. Replace the lie with God's love and His truth that will make you free. Then pass what you have learned onto the next generation.[5]

So Jesus said to the Jews who had believed him, "If you abide in my word, you are truly my disciples, and you will know the truth, and the truth will set you free." (John 8:31-32)

According to the KJV Application Study Bible Commentary, Jesus Himself is the truth that *makes* us free. John 8:36 says He is the source of truth and the perfect standard of what is right. God sets us free like a bird in a cage. He opens the door but we won't fly out. We just sit there and swing. He has to make us free by reaching in and grabbing us to make us free.

So if the Son sets you free, you will be free indeed. (John 8:36)

---

[5]   *Beyond Fear* by Nate Holcomb

Jesus does not give us freedom to do what we want, but freedom to follow God. As we seek to serve God, Jesus' perfect truth frees us to be all that God meant us to be. Then, we can be the example our children need to break these generational curses and instill a positive legacy into our children and our children's children.

A good man leaves an inheritance to his children's children, but the sinner's wealth is laid up for the righteous. (Proverbs 13:22)

Though eventually the path I took was toward the goal of a positive inheritance for my son and the next generation, I had a long way to go to get there. I thank God every day that He never gave up on me!

Poems from Prison

Concrete, steel, shackles, and chains,
Dreams of freedom so far away.

Black eyes, bloody noses,
Struggles and temptations.

Nothing compared to the price,
That was paid for my salvation.

- Anthony Monda

Broke, Busted, and Disgusted

Broke, busted, and disgusted, another druggy and I devised a plan to score some dope. My partner in crime was a distant family member who later died due to health issues. I drove us to his side of town to pull the "old bait and switch." He phoned ahead to set up the drug deal. The plan was to drive up and as soon as the dope was handed off, I would take off. That's what we did, but the only problem was the dealer latched on to the side of my car. He was holding on for dear life with a very angry look on his face.

My partner was a big dude, but he had a scared to death look on his face because things didn't go as planned. I yelled at him to punch the drug dealer in the face and then push him off my car, but to no avail. Astonished at the scared frozen state my partner was in, I actually thought he was going to start crying. Realizing he was not going to do anything about it, I figured it was now all on me to pullover and fight the guy or somehow shake him loose. Choosing the second option, I accelerated to about 40 miles an hour and started swerving back and forth.

Seeing an opportunity to knock him loose, I looked the dude in the eyes and pointed to an oncoming mailbox. Instead of letting go, he took that mailbox out with his body and still held on. Slamming him into one mailbox after another, he still refused to let go. Then all of a sudden I got his attention again and pointed to another oncoming mailbox. This one was made out of brick from the ground up. He held on to the very end and then finally let go. Driving off as fast as I could, I never looked back.

The things I did to feed my addiction like the sleepless nights, the days without food, walking for miles in the hot sun, begging for change, and stealing from people never did fulfill my real needs. We need the same tenacity that led me to do whatever it would take to fill my drug habit, to pursue the things of God. As Christians, we should hold fast to our faith no matter what kind of trouble we run into.

Can you remember the last time you prayed late into the night or fasted more than one meal? Have you gone door-to-door in the hot sun to tell someone about Jesus? It's time we go the extra mile and press toward the mark for the prize of the high calling of God in Christ Jesus with the same tenacity we used to pursue our sin (Philippians 3:14).

Evading arrest

One night, I was working out of town and stopped at a restaurant in Virginia for a bite to eat. I told myself that tonight I would get my act together. I would eat, drink, and be merry, but I would not do any crack. After a good meal and three alcohol-laced Long Island ice teas, I was off to the races. I jumped into the work van and sped off.

Out of nowhere, I saw blue lights flashing in my rear view mirror. My first thought was this would be my second DWI. My alcohol drugged mind was racing as I tried to come up with a plan to avoid arrest. *I have to jump out and make a run for it,* I thought and that's what I did.

I slammed the work van into park, and was out and running before the van came to a screeching stop. With a head start, the race was on. As I ran for my life, I heard their footsteps slowly fade behind me. I ran until I could run no more. Looking back, I saw no one so I decided to slide up under a parked car and wait it out as I tried to catch my breath. However, my heart was beating out of my chest and my gasping for air gave away my position. With guns drawn, they forced me to come out from under the car. I was arrested and charged with DWI and evading arrest. When we got to the police station, I got my one phone call. I called my girlfriend, the former sheriff's daughter. To my surprise, they let me go and I never heard anything more about it.

Another time, I parked near the train tracks and walked across them to score some crack like I had done a hundred times before. On my way back across the tracks with crack in hand, I was surprised by two police officers who jumped out from behind a parked caboose. Following my first instinct, I ran, but it was dark and several train tracks were in my way. As I tried to hurdle the tracks and gain speed, I got tripped up and fell across the tracks dropping the crack. About that time, I felt an officer's night stick come down full force across my back. Foolishly, I jumped to my feet, took off again, and tripped over the very next set of tracks. Again I got the officer's night stick to the back. They say third time is a charm, so I got up again, I ran, I fell, I got the stick, and I went to jail. However, the crack was lost somewhere near my first fall and police dogs couldn't sniff it out so I was let go for lack of evidence.

Pistol Whipped

Though most of my friends and family wanted nothing to do with me, there were times I'd be allowed to stay with my sister Micca. One night, I am ashamed to say, I stole several checks out of her purse, forged her name, and cashed them at a local market to buy crack. Then I drove down to the projects, stopped the first person I saw standing on the street corner that looked like a drug dealer, and told him what I wanted and how much. Suddenly, I had a gun stuck in my face and the man demanded my money. My addiction was so strong, I was not giving up my money unless I got my drugs even at gun point.

Desperately trying to get my standard transmission car out of neutral, I sat grinding gears in an attempt to make a fast get away. Not so easy from a dead stop, I was not fast enough and took a blow to the forehead from the gun barrel. Blood immediately started running down my face and into my eyes. I finally got the car in first gear, laid over in the seat, and drove off as fast as I could finding my way against the curb in fear the guy might decide to pull the trigger.

Strung out and with blood streaming down my face, I continued my search to feed my addiction. Occasionally wiping the blood from my

Thank God that today I am covered by the blood of Jesus. Now when God looks at me, He sees Jesus and not the messed up drug addict I used to be.

eyes so I could see enough to drive, I finally scored and headed back to my sister's house.

Fortunately, Micca was already in bed when I arrived, so I went straight to the bathroom, shut the door, and locked it. Looking in the mirror at the blood covering my face, I watched myself smoke the crack until it was all gone. The effects of the high caused me to search the entire bathroom for more. Not until I was convinced there was no more crack did I clean the blood from my face.

We can be in an environment or culture where God is not acknowledged, but thank God He is never absent. He will find us wherever we are and protect us even from ourselves.

Oh, what joy for those
whose disobedience is forgiven,
whose sin is put out of sight!
Yes, what joy for those
whose record the Lord *has cleared of guilt*
whose lives are lived in complete honesty!
When I refused to confess my sin,
my body wasted away,
and I groaned all day long.
Day and night your hand of discipline was heavy on me.
My strength evaporated like water in the summer heat. (Psalm 32:1-4 NLT)

Poems from Prison

Chest out, chin up,
Eyes always open.

Got to stay together
Vultures looking for the broken.

Another day starts,
Another chance given,

To let His light shine in
In the way that I'm living.

- Anthony Monda

Chapter 3

Growing Up Spiritually

*And so, from the day we heard, we have not ceased to pray for you, asking that you may **be filled with the knowledge of his will in all spiritual wisdom and understanding.*** (Colossians 1:9 emphasis added)

Growing up spiritually is where I kept missing it. God always shows us the natural so we will understand the spiritual. For example, in school, you cannot graduate to the next level without a passing grade. You can't drive a car or get a job until you are of age and are mature enough to handle the responsibilities. The Bible says, "The heir, as long as he is a child, is no different from a slave, though he is the owner of everything, but he is under guardians and managers until the date set by his father" (Galatians 4:1-2).

God wants us to grow up spiritually and the Bible speaks about the three calls that move us through this growing up process. The **heavenly call** is a call to salvation. The **holy call** is a call to separation, and the **high call** is a call to sonship, servanthood.

*Therefore, holy brothers, you who share in a **heavenly calling**, consider Jesus, the apostle and high priest of our confession.* (Hebrews 3:1 emphasis added)

In Matthew 22:14, Jesus said, "For many are called, but few are chosen." The reason that few are chosen is because some never accept the call that is given in Romans 10:9, "That if you confess with your mouth and believe in your heart that 'Jesus is Lord' and that Jesus died on the cross for your sins and God raised him from the dead on the third day you are saved." If you have already done this, congratulations, you've answered and accepted the first call. If not, it is time you answer the **heavenly call** which is a call to salvation. When you answer this call, you are born again spiritually and become a newborn baby Christian.

*Therefore do not be ashamed of the testimony about our Lord, nor of me his prisoner, but share in suffering for the gospel by the power of God, who saved us and called us to a **holy calling**, not because of our works but because of his own purpose and grace, which he gave us in Christ Jesus before the ages began.* (2 Timothy 1:8-9 emphasis added)

Once you are saved, God wants you to move forward and begin to grow up through prayer, Bible study, and not forsaking fellowship with other believers (Hebrews 10:25). This will empower you to answer and succeed in the **holy call**, the call to separate yourself from the things of this world, from the old you, and from things that are not pleasing to God. Ephesians 4:24 says, "Put on the new self, created after the likeness of God in true righteousness and holiness." 1 John 2:15 warns, "Do not love the world or the things in the world. If anyone loves the world, the love of the Father is not in him." In Romans 1:1, the apostle Paul introduces himself as, "a servant of Christ Jesus, called to be an apostle, **set apart** for the gospel of God." We are each called to be set apart to do the kingdom work that God has equipped us to do.

*I press toward the mark for the prize of the **high calling** of God in Christ Jesus.* (KJV Philippians 3:14 emphasis added)

There is the **high call** to sonship and servanthood. In other words, at this point you are stepping into maturity and can handle the responsibilities you have been given by the Father. You know it's not about you anymore. You stop asking what's in it for you and realize it's all about loving God and loving God's people. 1 Corinthians 13:11 says, "When I was a child, I spoke like a child, I thought like a child, I reasoned like a child. When I became a man, I gave up childish ways."

The apostle Peter is a great example of moving through this process as he went from a reed, to a stone, and then to becoming a pillar in God's kingdom. When Jesus first called Peter He called him Simon which means "reed." A reed is shallow and weak and represents immaturity. Peter means "stone," which represents placement. We find our place in God. A pillar is symbolic of a mature Christian anointed, supportive, righteous, and strong under pressure who is filled with wisdom. He went from the **heavenly calling**, to the **holy calling**, and on to the **high calling** of God in Christ Jesus. That is the path to spiritual growth we are all to take as well.

It has been said that God will call your name once and you will hear it for the rest of your life like an echo until you answer it or until you die. When God calls your name, how will you respond? Will you brush it off believing you are hearing things? Will you dismiss it and go on with whatever you were doing? One thing is for sure, God is calling you. It is time you answer the call.

The AA/NA Halfway House

One of the many times I reached out for help, I committed myself to a six-month AA program and was allowed to live in a halfway house, though it was not free. I had to pay rent, so I got a job working across the street from the halfway house. The deal was if I stayed clean six months, the rent money would be given back to me and then I could get my own place. Though I was excited about the opportunity of what I thought God had provided for me, I was operating in my own strength.

Looking back, I think it was so ironic that where I was staying was called a halfway house. For me, it was symbolic of my spiritual growth. I had one foot in God and one foot in world. I was half-baked, meaning I was going through the motions, acting as if I didn't have a clue, I was riding the fence.

In Matthew 15:8 Jesus warned, "This people honors me with their lips, but their heart is far from me." When we claim to honor God while our hearts are far from Him, our worship means nothing. It is not enough to "act religious." Our actions, our desires, and our attitudes must be sincerely focused on God and pleasing to Him. Mind you, I was consistently going to

I was honoring God with my lips, but my heart was far from Him.

AA meetings as well as to church on Sundays. AA was mandatory in the six-month rehab program, but not church. I went to church anyways because I knew that's where God really wanted me, but I was still always trying to take the easy path. I felt good about myself and confident I would never use drugs again. Smoking crack was the farthest thing from my mind. I prayed, read my Bible occasionally, and attended several different area churches, gleaning information from each one. Life was good. I was good. Life couldn't be any better.

At the very first AA meeting I went to, God spoke to me through the testimony of one of the speakers. After the man confessed he was an alcoholic and had been several years sober, he went on to say it's not the big book or the people who keep him sober or the meetings.

He emphatically declared, "It is God who keeps me sober." Right then and there I knew God was speaking to me that I was supposed to be in church getting to know Him and get to know Him I did!

I learned that confession is powerful. The Bible says there is death and life in the power of the tongue. God doesn't call me a drug addict so why should I call me a drug addict? God calls me a new creation. God calls me friend. God calls me an overcomer, a mighty man of valor, and so does my iPhone Siri because I told her to. Words **are** powerful!

I worked hard and made it five months into the program. I could see the end in sight as I was just a few weeks away from getting all my money back and was looking forward to getting my own place. Then my income tax refund check came in the mail. Across the street was a car dealership that sold cars that had been repossessed. One of my goals was to buy a car, so I was in hog heaven when I found I had enough to buy one. The last thing on my mind was messing it all up. As a matter of fact, I had even said, "I feel confident I will never use again."

I found the perfect car and bought it from the dealership. Then I bought some cleaning supplies and began to clean the interior of my new car. The car was very dirty and there was trash everywhere. All the doors had side pockets so I worked my way around, cleaning all the trash out of the pockets. When I got to the pocket in the passenger side door, I pulled out a baggie that looked like it had crack cocaine inside.

Without thinking and with no hesitation, I kicked into autopilot. As I had done so many times in the past, I opened the bag, reached inside, and pulled out the little white rock. Then I tasted it to see if it was real. It was and instantly I ran into the halfway house desperately searching for a soda can or something that I could make a pipe out of. Within a few minutes of finding the crack, I was smoking it. Off to the races I went, chasing the high all day long and empting my bank account in the process.

However, when the binge was over, there was nothing left for me to do except face the consequences of what I done. The next phase of the enemy's attack was to hit me with severe condemnation. The enemy of our soul has a plot and a plan to keep us out there in the world and away from those who can help us, especially when we fall. Like always he used my habitual back-

God brings conviction to our hearts when we do something wrong, but the devil brings condemnation to make us feel like there is no hope of forgiveness and restoration.

sliding to condemn me and try to keep me from getting back up and trying again.

*There is therefore now **no condemnation** for those who are in Christ Jesus.* (Romans 8:1 emphasis added)

The Application Study Bible commentary on Matthew 12:43-45 says, "Just cleaning up one's life without filling it up with God leaves plenty of room for Satan to enter. Ridding our lives of sin is the first step. We must also take the second step, filling our lives with God's Word and the Holy Spirit. 7Unfilled and complacent people are easy targets for Satan."

"When an evil spirit leaves a person, it goes into the desert, seeking rest but finding none. Then it says, 'I will return to the person I came from.' So it returns and finds its former home empty, swept, and clean. Then the spirit finds seven other spirits more evil than itself, and they all enter the person and live there. And so that person is worse off than before." (Matthew 12:43-45)

The world says once a crack head always a crack head, but God says in 2 Corinthians 5:17, "If any man be in Christ he is a new creation old things are passed away; behold, all things are become new." Today, I am a brand-new man on the inside. The Holy Spirit has given me new life, and I am not the same anymore. I am not reformed, rehabilitated, or reeducated I am a new creation, living in vital union with Christ. I have not merely turned over a new leaf, I am beginning a new life under a new master. However, before I reached this point, I had to go through a little more boot camp. There was more to my spiritual growth process. I still had an issue with foolish stinking pride that kept me from truly and fully turning my life over to God.

Foolish Stinking Pride

For ever since the world was created, people have seen the earth and sky. Through everything God made, they can clearly see his invisible qualities—his eternal power and divine nature. So they have no excuse for not knowing God.

Yes, they knew God, but they wouldn't worship him as God or even give him thanks. And they began to think up foolish ideas of what God was like. As a result, their minds became dark and confused. Claiming to be wise, they instead became utter fools. And instead of worshiping the glorious, ever-living God, they worshiped idols made to look like mere people and birds and animals and reptile. So God abandoned them to do whatever shameful things their hearts desired. (Romans 1:20-24 NLT emphasis added)

Like those people described in Romans 1:20-24, I chose to reject God and God allowed me to do it. God does not usually stop us from making choices even if they are against His will. He lets us declare our own supposed independence from Him, even though He knows that in time we will become slaves to our own rebellious choices and lose our freedom to sin.

After the beat down that left me with broken ribs, a broken nose, and a broken tooth, I went into the Teen Challenge program in Nashville, Tennessee. I knew now for sure that I could not do this on my own. I needed the structure and protection being in and around men and women of God in order to stay strong and resist the pull of the world. I was there a couple weeks before they shipped me off to San Antonio, Texas. I was there a couple years and was promoted from student to a paid position. My title was resident intern. That's when God began pushing me out of my comfort zone. Humiliation came to see if I would humble myself so God could honor me.

The fear of the LORD *is instruction in wisdom, and humility comes before honor.* (Proverbs 15:33)

However, even after all the rehabs, all the spiritual growth centers, and all the beat downs I had been through, I was still full of pride. The Bible says we are to obey those who have a rule over us and make their job easy for them. I had not yet learned the value of this important principle in moving forward in my spiritual growth.

Have confidence in your leaders and submit to their authority, because they keep watch over you as those who must give an account. Do this so that their work will be a joy, not a burden, for that would be of no benefit to you. (Hebrews 13:17 NIV)

I can't remember when or how it all began, but two years into the program at Teen Challenge, I began to butt heads with the director. It felt like he was out to get me and to make my life miserable. It got so bad I went to the executive director to let him know that I was being unfairly treated. He simply quoted 1 Corinthians 10:13, "There is no temptation taken you but such as is common to man that God is faithful and he will not allow you to suffer above what ye are able and with every temptation he will always leave you a way of escape."

Iron sharpens iron and one man sharpens another. (Proverbs 27:17)

At the time, though I was now in my forties, I was immature and unlearned so quoting scripture just didn't do it for me. I felt like everybody was against me. *Who do they think they are? I'm not a doormat,* I thought to myself day after day. My attitude was so bad that shortly after that discussion with the executive director, I made a comment that got back to him and I was called out on the carpet. After going back and forth with him, I told him that he might as well put a millstone around about his neck and be cast in the deep sea for causing one of God's baby Christians to stumble. He replied back at me saying I was not a baby Christian.

Turning toward the door, I said, "Compared to you I am."

Arrogantly walking out of his office, I claimed to myself that I had just been used by the Holy Ghost to put the director in his place.

However, all it really did was get me stripped of my internship, my leadership position, and my pay. As a resident intern, I had received free room and board and a small amount of pay weekly. Disgruntled and mad at the world and everybody in it, without praying or thinking about what I was doing, I moved out. Though I was not kicked out of the program, I felt I had no other choice but to start looking for another job and another place to live. I can't remember if I ever got a job, but I do remember it didn't take long before I was smoking crack again.

God's Way, the Right Way

Sometimes, the way of a man seems right at the time, but in the end it would lead to poverty instead of prosperity (Proverbs 14:12, 16:25). I've

As I look back, I realize God allowed that situation at Teen Challenge to kill my pride.

learned that God will use the positive and negative in our lives to grow us. Just like a car battery has positive and negative to make a car start, God will purposely put positive and negative people in our everyday lives to get us started and keep us moving in the right direction. Most of us think we know what's best for us, when in fact we are being foolish.

For the foolishness of God is wiser than men, and the weakness of God is stronger than men. For consider your calling, brothers: not many of you were wise according to worldly standards, not many were powerful, not many were of noble birth. But God chose what is foolish in the world to shame the wise; God chose what is weak in the world to shame the strong; God chose what is low and despised in the world, even things that are not, to bring to nothing things that are, so that no human being might boast in the presence of God. (1 Corinthians 1:25-29)

God never calls perfect people, only people who are willing to do as He leads. The résumé for being used by Christ is to be what the world considers foolish and weak. When the devil sends his best, God messes the devil up with a mess up like me. Today, my mess has become my message. God uses who He chooses, not who the world says is qualified. God didn't leave me a fool. He has made me wise by giving me the mind of Christ. Even if the world sees me as foolish and weak, all that matters is what God thinks. His plan is a plan of good and not evil (Jeremiah 29:11). I can expect God to keep on healing me, keep on delivering me, keep on rescuing me, keep on blessing me, and keep on showing me what I need to know to grow. The more I learn about God, the more I realize what I don't know. The closer I get to God the more I see how far away I actually am. God tells us in His word:

My people are destroyed for lack of knowledge. (Hosea 4:6)

My advice to you is that no matter how uncomfortable it may seem at the time, let God push you out of your comfort zone into His plan for your life. Then you will experience God's promises and truly live the life He has designed for you to live. God is not a respecter of persons. He is a respecter of faith. Remember one very important truth, with God all things are possible (Matthew 19:26).

Ask Yourself. . .

- *Have I truly and fully turned my life over to God?*
- *Have I allowed the Holy Spirit to do the spiritual house cleaning that needs to be done in my thinking, my attitude, and my actions?*

- *How is my relationship with those in authority over me?*

- *What changes is God asking me to make in my life right now to correct some of these issues?*

SAMMinistries

I was accepted into the SAMMinistries Living and Learning Center which is a homeless shelter for families and single parents. I know that it was God because I had not been clean very long and yet they still accepted me.

It was at SAMM that I met my future wife, Melody. Now, I would not recommend that if you're looking for a wife to look in the homeless shelter, but God does use what appears to be the foolish things of this world to confound the wise. Though Melody and I were the complete opposite of each other and she got on my nerves in the beginning, we became friends and talked quite frequently. She lived right down the hall from me and we both were in the college program. We did have one other thing in common, we both claimed to be Christians. Of course, I was struggling spiritually and I found she was struggling with issues of her own. Anyway, in college I had many papers due and I was an inept two-finger typist. Melody offered to type my papers.

Though I was on the right track, I still hadn't grown up which is where a lot of Christians miss it. I took some steps in the right direction, but then I would revert to trying to do things in my own strength.

Sister Ernestine, the director of SAMMinistries Living and Learning Center, once said, "Barry Monda sure does fall a lot, but there's one thing about him, he always gets right back up."

Even when everybody saw the worst in me, God saw the best in me. So even though I fell several times in the process of trying to get clean, I got back up again and again. Thankfully, God always had someone there to be His spokesman to help guide me back on the right path.

After about a year in the SAMMinistries Living and Learning Center two-year program, I fell again. However, God was still in control and somehow I was accepted into AmeriCorps and got to stay at the downtown homeless shelter for transients. There I lived off school loans as I attempted to get my associate degree as a Licensed Chemical Dependency Counselor. Still working on my issues, I was almost there and already counseling at the B.E.A.T. A.I.D.S. Outreach Center as an intern when I fell again.

Stuck on Stupid - Death Angel Knocking at My Door

Leaving the homeless shelter, I ended up staying in a cheap motel where I had been smoking crack nonstop for several days. Stuck on stupid, I had gone without food or drink the whole time which lead me to having a near-death experience. I had smoked so much crack it was seeping up out of the pores of my head in tiny bubbles of residue. I remember being delirious, very weak, and when I looked around I could not focus because everything was a blur. Definitely in zombie mode, I should have been dead, but somehow I was still alive.

Sitting on the bed like a statue staring at the TV, I couldn't even see the numbers on the remote I was holding in my hand. I was just randomly clicking through the channels. All of a sudden, Joel Osteen was looking back at me from the TV screen. Instantly, I was relaxed, didn't feel sick or at the point of death anymore. I could see the TV screen very clearly and was in my right mind.

Joel turned, looked directly into the camera at me, and said, "I feel the presence of the Lord."

God was there with me in that motel room. That's the moment God began to rebuke me about running away from my problems and letting my feelings get the best of me. God was telling me it was time for me to grow up and be the man He had called me to be. Once I'd heard the message, my vision blurred again, I became tense, cramped up, sick, and out of my mind. The death angel was at my door!

Just then, for some reason the person that had been bringing me the crack cut me off and brought me food and drink instead. Aware the death angel was knocking at my door, I forced myself to eat. However, while I was eating, I began to hallucinate. Someone pulled up a chair and began to encourage me. As I watched, the face of this person changed into different people that I looked up to and admired. Then I saw three more people enter the room. One sat by the front door as if to guard it from intruders. Every so often one of them would give me a tiny piece of crack to smoke to ease my suffering and slowly bring me back to life and a sense of normalcy. I don't know how long this process went on, but I truly believe God saved me that day from certain death and sent His angels to battle the death angel.

I can never escape from your Spirit!
I can never get away from your presence
If I go up to heaven, you are there;
if I go down to the grave, you are there.
If I ride the wings of the morning,
if I dwell by the farthest oceans,
even there your hand will guide me,
and your strength will support me.
I could ask the darkness to hide me
and the light around me to become night—
but even in darkness I cannot hide from you.
To you the night shines as bright as day.
Darkness and light are the same to you.
(Psalm 139:7-12 NLT)

After I backslid again, my caseworker at the homeless shelter introduced me to her husband who was in AA. She got him to take me to a church where he thought they had AA and NA meetings. He was wrong. It turns out that he took me exactly where I needed to be, Victory Gospel Chapel and Spiritual Growth Center. We call it "the home." It was a divine appointment where they taught me biblical principles that changed my life.

Instead of running from God, we need to come to ourselves and run back toward Him.

Though we may try to blame other people for hurting us, or our experiences in life that have taken what we hold dear from us, or our boss for not understanding us, sin is the real culprit. We need to turn to God, confess our sins, and allow Him to cleanse us and make us whole.

If we say we have no sin, we deceive ourselves, and the truth is not in us. If we confess our sins, he is faithful and just to forgive us our sins and to cleanse us from all unrighteousness. If we say we have not sinned, we make him a liar, and his word is not in us. (1 John 1:8-10)

Ask Yourself. . .

- *Am I running from God instead of toward Him?*
- *What am I running away from or to?*
- *Who or what am I blaming for my sin?*
- *Am I making God a liar by refusing to confess my sin?*

Will you turn to God today, confess your sins, and allow Him to cleanse you from all unrighteousness?

Poems from Prison

Start it out right,
Bend to my knees,

Pray for a mind renewed,
Let Jesus take the lead.

Ready to face the day,
Walk by faith not by sight,

I pray without ceasing
Ready for the fight.

-Anthony Monda

Victory Gospel Chapel Poster

Chapter 4

Victory Gospel Chapel

The Un-cut Gospel

Victory Gospel Chapel is a church that preaches and teaches the uncut gospel—the death, the burial, and the resurrection of Christ Jesus. Bishop Donny and Prophetess Jackie Banks, also founded the Spiritual Growth Center, a place for people with life controlling problems like me. Prayer and Bible classes are held three times a day there with church on Sunday morning, Sunday night, and Wednesday night. Hardly ever does a week go by that there is not some type of conference being held at VGC as well.

I was about to learn that God doesn't give up on backsliders. He talks to us even when we are in sin and a backslidden condition. He reminded me of His Word that says going back I would become seven times worse. He also warned me of becoming reprobate meaning rejected by God. I wanted to come back to God but couldn't.

Since they thought it foolish to acknowledge God, he abandoned them to their foolish thinking (reprobate KJV) *and let them do things that should never be done. Their lives became full of every kind of wickedness, sin, greed, hate, envy, murder, quarreling, deception, malicious behavior, and gossip. They are backstabbers, haters of God, insolent, proud, and boastful. They invent new ways of sinning, and they disobey their parents. They refuse to understand, break their promises, are heartless, and have no mercy. They know God's justice requires that those who do these things deserve to die, yet they do them anyway. Worse yet, they encourage others to do them, too.* (Romans 1:28-32 NLT)

"I'm Going to Get Help!"

For one long year I did nothing but smoke crack. Like I said I wanted to come back but couldn't. I had turned my back on God and He turned me over to my sin. Though I frustrated the grace of God, He did not give up on me. He is the God of second chances. One day I learned an important lesson about turning to God for help from a secular rehab.

They blindfolded us, loaded us into a van, and drove us out into the country. Then they led us to the top of a hill where we were told to grab hold of a rope that was about waist high. We were then told that we were in a maze and to follow the rope until we found our way out. If we had any questions we could stop and raise our hand.

We had barely gotten started when I heard the announcement that someone had found **the way** out of the maze. Then we heard that two or three more people had found **the way** out. Eventually, those of us that had not found **the way** out were told to remove our blindfolds. To my surprise, the rope went around four or five trees in a complete circle with no end and no way out. Then we were told that those who stopped, raised their hand, and asked for help were the ones who had found **the way** out of the maze.

Jesus told him, "I am the way, the truth, and the life. No one can come to the Father except through me. (John 14:6 NLT)

God is a God of many chances, and His grace abounds for as much as we need it, and His mercies are new every morning. His peace surpasses all understanding. His joy is unspeakable, but believe me when I say you do not want to frustrate the grace of God!

I can remember the day God released crack's hold on me. I ran all the way *home*, about five blocks, to Victory Gospel Chapel's Spiritual Growth Center. On the way, I passed the dope man who yelled to get my attention.

I yelled back without breaking my stride, "I'm going to get help."

Believe it or not he actually cheered me on.

Last Chance/Final Training Ground

When I arrived at the "home," the Spiritual Growth Center, they lead me in the sinner's prayer and ministered to my physical needs.

They fed me and gave me a bed to sleep in. After a couple days of rest they began to work on me spiritually. The first service I attended, I was sitting right in the front row. When I looked up, Bishop Donny Banks looked like a giant. The anointing was so strong I knew without a shadow of a doubt that I was where I was supposed to be. The peace was amazing as God's healing and deliverance began taking place in my life through hearing and hearing and hearing God's Word through the daily preaching and teaching at the Spiritual Growth Center.

I could hear God's still small voice telling me this was my last chance and my final training ground. He was leading me to make a commitment and a decision to surrender all. He wanted me to step into His plan for my life. I was definitely sick and tired of being sick and tired, so I made a decision and committed to myself and to the Lord to follow His plan for my life.

"Whatever you want me to do Lord, I'll do," like I had said many times before and always really meant it.

When I arrived at the Spiritual Growth Center, I just wanted to stop smoking crack. I just wanted to have a normal life. The Spiritual Growth Center was free, supplying beds, three meals a day, clothes, and work release accountability. You can stay as long as you need to get your life in order. However, the Spiritual Growth Center was different than all the other centers I had been in. They didn't just teach me the Word of God, they actually put me in a position to begin applying it to my life. We were placed as ushers and parking lot attendants to work for God. It felt good to be doing something constructive with my life and give back to the God who had forgiven me and saved me from myself.

At VGC, they also launch churches and spiritual growth centers and God uses people like me to do His work. As I saw what they did there and how people were changed through actually participating, I began to dream of not only a normal life, but a life of service to God. I thought perhaps God was calling me to go into full-time ministry, stepping out by faith, and starting a church and spiritual growth center. Dreaming big, I knew I couldn't do it on my own, but I knew God could if that was what He wanted me to do. I was on fire for the Lord wanting nothing more than to please Him.

One Sunday morning as I was working as a parking lot attendant, the pastor's wife walked by. I was still excited about my call to full time ministry and I boldly announced that I was called to full time ministry.

She replied even bolder, "First, let's see if you can keep a job and pay some bills."

I was on a spiritual high and needed to be grounded. Actually, I was kind of relieved I was going to work first and that God had given such insight to those called as my oversight. I was learning to pray, hear from God, and then get conformation from the men and women of God He placed over me before making any important decision.

Although several times in my past I felt the same way and even said I felt confident I'll never use again, this time something was different. I couldn't quite put my finger on it, but something had changed. Maybe it was the fullness of time, but this time I was willing to do whatever it takes to get my life in order. I wanted everything that God had for me.

Testimony Day

In Revelation 12:11, the Bible confirms that we overcomers by the blood of the Lamb and by the word of our testimony. So, after thirty days in the Spiritual Growth Center program, we are encouraged to give our testimonies. Testifying, ushering, greeting and parking lot attending was just the beginning. God wants us to find something for our hands to do (Ecclesiastes 9:10), and find our place in Him. A man's gift makes room for him, and brings him before great men (Proverbs 18:16). Finding my gift was not so easy because though I thought I had made a total commitment to God, the spirit of fear came upon me worse than any stage fright. The last thing I wanted to do was stand up in front of a crowd of people and speak.

Not that I didn't want to talk about what I'd done and where I'd been. I actually thought I was dumb and stupid and would never amount to anything and didn't want to take the risk of freezing up and being laughed at. Just thinking about it caused my blood pressure to sky rocket to the point of hyperventilation. So I decided to do 29 days and skedaddle. I didn't feel ready and wasn't equipped to fight the weight of my world.

God knew what I was battling and during the preaching of the Word He reminded me He had me right where I was supposed to be and these were the things I was supposed to do. I believe because I had begun to develop a prayer life and had been hearing the Word of God preached and taught, my faith had increased. As I tried to prepare myself for testimony day, I memorized all the scriptures I could find about dealing with fear.

For God has not given us a spirit of fear, but of power and of love and of a sound mind. (2 Timothy 1:7 NKJV)

The wicked flee when no one pursues,
But the righteous are bold as a lion.
(Proverbs 28:1 NKJV)

For you did not receive the spirit of bondage again to fear, but you received the Spirit of adoption by whom we cry out. . ." . . .Daddy, God! (Romans 8:15 NKJV)

And when they had prayed, the place where they were assembled together was shaken; and they were all filled with the Holy Spirit, and they spoke the word of God with boldness. (Acts 4:31 NKJV)

I memorized all these scriptures and more, but I was still afraid. I prayed and asked God to take away my fear and give me a boldness to do what He was asking me to do. I talked to one of the elders at the church about my dilemma. He told me we will always feel that terrifying feeling because the devil whispers in our ear saying we're dumb and stupid and we can't do it. God's not going to take that away he said, but all I have to remember is that God didn't give it to me. He gave me power, love, and a sound mind. Easier said than done. It wasn't easy facing the cold hard fact of the matter, some things God will not remove. He tells me in His Word that His grace is sufficient. He says when I am weak then I am strong. As I continued to grow, eventually like the apostle Paul I learned to be glad and boast about my weakness (2 Corinthians 12:9-11). Even to this day, God uses my weakness to keep me humble and show Himself strong.

Courage is fear that has said its prayers. - Dorothy Bernard

So, my thirtieth day in the program arrived and I was called on to give my testimony. Immediately, I felt stressed to the max. I could feel the heat and I began to sweat. It was just like the elder said. The terrifying feeling and voices were still there. Everything intensified, but I got up and made my way to the front of class. I stumbled and staggered through my testimony and made my way back to my seat still in a state of shock. It was definitely a step out of my comfort zone, a big step, a giant step, a gigantic step. After that, every class during testimony time, I would raise my hand. I had learned how to fight and decided to give the devil a black eye every chance I got. At the same time, I was learning to overcome my fear by operating in faith. I did it so often that they finally stopped calling on me.

And He said to me, "My grace is sufficient for you, for My strength is made perfect in weakness." Therefore most gladly I will rather boast in my infirmities, that the power of Christ may rest upon me. Therefore I take pleasure in infirmities, in reproaches, in needs, in persecutions, in distresses, for Christ's sake. For when I am weak, then I am strong. (2 Corinthians12:9-10 NKJV)

I never actually got comfortable testifying, but because I stepped out of my comfort zone and trusted God, now when it's my turn to testify, teach, preach, or witness, I go and do what God calls me to do. Now, I know that the fear will leave me and the Holy Spirit will come in and help me. Like Paul, who prayed three times for God to take away the thorn in his side, I prayed many times for God to take away that terrifying feeling. Like God told Paul, He told me, "My grace is sufficient for you, for my power is made perfect in weakness" (2 Corinthians 12:9 NIV). Because of where God's taking me, I need the thorn in my side to keep me humble so I won't ever think I'm "all that and a bag of chips." We are overcomers by the blood of the Lamb and by the word of our testimony.

Today, I understand the reason God left that thorn in my side. It was to keep me humble so that He could move me where He wanted me to go. Today, God has blessed me with a holy wife, taken me from being homeless to a home owner, from unemployed to an employer, from a crack head to a youth pastor and elder. Soon I will be a published author of a best seller that points to Jesus who is the author and finisher of my faith, the hope of glory, who heals, who sets free, and who delivers others like He has me (Colossians 1:27).

Les Brown said, "Too many of us are not living our dreams because we are living our fears."

After thirty days at the center, I saw how God also used fundraising in my transformation. When they said "fundraising" I heard pan handling. As soon as those thoughts came into my mind I said to myself, "I'm not begging people for money." Right then and there God reminded me that I did it for my addiction. Now I get three hot meals a day, clothes, shelter, and best of all the priceless Word of God all free. How could I say no? I used to hold a sign standing on the interstate off-ramp that read "hungry." The sad truth was I was hungry for more drugs. . . crack, but today I'm hungry for the things of God. Today I hunger and thirst for righteousness. Today I hunger for lost souls.

I can remember how fundraising helped me. I was used to spending any money I had in my pocket on crack. At times while fundraising I had up to $100 in my pocket and never once had the uncontrollable urge to go spend it on crack. This was a good feeling. I know it was not by might, not by power, but by His spirit.

Jail Time

I can remember one time a training leader and I were arrested for outstanding warrants while fundraising. Immediately, the training leader I was with lost all hope and begin to murmur and complain. Even though he had been there longer and been promoted to training leader, he was only in his twenties with very little street experience. I guess you could say I had my mind made up and my heart was fixed after a number of setbacks. I had decided to go with Jesus all the way no matter what. I began to encourage the training leader by saying we made a decision to live for Jesus and we were in right standing with God now. Therefore, if we're going to jail it is because somebody there needs to hear that Jesus loves them and cares about what happens to them. We were being sent by God to tell them there was a place they can go to learn more about Jesus when they get out of jail. To me, it was an opportunity God had orchestrated for us to accomplish His purpose in someone else's life.

As a matter of fact, I testified all the way to jail to the policeman driving us. When we got there, the holding cells were three separate chain-link fences stretching all the way to the ceiling. They unlocked the gate and put us in the middle one. Because they were chain-link fences you could see everybody in the other cages left and right. I never stopped encouraging my training leader. I told him that we were there for a reason and to tell someone about Jesus. With my red and white Jesus fundraising T-shirt on, I began to testify to the first person sitting on the bench. Then I looked up at the training leader, raised my finger indicating "that's one." I slid over to the next person and begin to testify about Jesus. I can remember looking up at him again and held up two fingers. "That's two!" I tried to encourage him to do the same as I went from person to person.

All of a sudden, I realized I was standing in the middle of the fenced-in cell though I don't know how I got there. However, I had everyone's attention. Everybody was looking at me in the cell we were in and in the cells on either side of me. God had taken over completely. The undeniable overwhelming presence of the Lord was there.

Looking around I said to everyone, "Man, I feel the Holy Ghost! You've got to feel it, too!"

Everybody had this look of expectancy on their face. At that moment, the guard called out my name. He handcuffed me to another guy and took us to another room in the back to see if we could get out on our own recognizance.

As the officer lead me away, I was laughing. Of course I've never been drunk in the Holy Ghost before. I had only heard about it. I remember laughing trying to explain to the guard why I felt so good and what just happened. The guard sat me down in front of a lady who sat behind a protected glass booth trying to ask me questions, but I couldn't shut up about what just happened. Believe it or not they let me go on my own recognizance and they kept the training leader.

So always remember no matter what situation you might be in or how out of place it might seem you could be on an assignment from God. My prayer is to come into agreement with Jabez.

Jabez' prayer:

"Oh, that You would bless me indeed, and enlarge my territory, that Your hand would be with me, and that You would keep me from evil, that I may not cause pain!"(1 Chron 4:10 NKJV) (paraphrased) . . .God give me more responsibility and opportunities to touch more souls for Your glory.

Sometimes I question the Lord, why me? I am reminded of my prayer.

my prayer. "Here I am, Lord, send me (Isaiah 6:8). I'll stand in the gap (Ezekiel 22:30). I'll tell someone about You."

Ask Yourself. . .

- *What fear am I facing that is keeping me from doing what God has called me to do?*
- *Which of the scripture verses in this chapter ministered to me the most?*
- *Will I take a stand today and face that fear and begin to do what God has called me to do?*

Poems from Prison

All of my struggles

All of my fears

Every hurt

Every tear

Led me to You hoping You could bare

The ugliness of me and show me You care.

I was always confused and never could see

What I was doing wrong that made my father always leave

Temporary placements with most of my family

Never lasted long I figured they couldn't stand me.

Foster care to group homes cigarettes to weed

Embracing worldly solutions that were only momentarily achieved.

-Anthony Monda

Chapter 5

With God All Things Are Possible

When the Israelites were fleeing from Pharaoh's army

God was not restricted by the Red Sea;

When Blind Bartimaeus was begging by the roadside

Jesus was not restricted by a disability;

Whenever we face an insurmountable situation

God is not restricted by our limitations.

We must not restrict God by our limitations.

God can and does do the impossible.[6]

But Jesus looked at them and said, "With man this is impossible, but with God all things are possible." (Matthew 19:26)

---

[6] http://daily-devotional.org/daily-devotions/all-things-are-possible/

Marriage, Family, and Our Own Business

In November of 2004, when I was forty-four years old, Melody and I got married. We were living in San Antonio and I was working construction. It was the rainy season in San Antonio, so I was only working maybe one or two days a week. They had also promised me a raise which I never got making me frustrated, disillusioned, and hard to get along with. We had only been married for about a month when I came home from a particularly frustrating day at work. I found Melody in our bedroom packing suitcases.

When I asked her where she was going she said, "I'm not going anywhere. You are. You are going back in 'the home'."

She was right. I had lost all my peace and joy. So, I humbled myself and got a new attitude by taking my eyes off my work situation and putting them back on Jesus. Soon the weather changed and there was plenty of work. I had been in the caulking and waterproofing business since I was nineteen years old. So, when it came to caulking and waterproofing I thought nobody could out-caulk me. I considered caulking an artform and felt no one can match my masterpieces when it came to caulking and waterproofing. I was faster, smoother, and more experienced than most.

The company I worked for won a big project. The company hired several workers and part of the contract was that every day sections of the work would be inspected. I was just one of the caulkers. The supervisor was a Christian so I had favor with him. He even talked about promoting me to lead man. A few weeks went by and the company promoted one of the other workers to lead man instead of me. This gentleman was not a caulker or a waterproofer. He was a beginner who also had favor with the supervisor because they went to church together.

One afternoon as we were cleaning up and getting ready to go the new project site, the newly appointed lead man called us all together and said to me, "I regret to inform you that you are being terminated."

My first reaction was to laugh and look around because I really thought he was joking. Fire me, the best, the fastest, and the smoothest caulker of them all? There was silence in the circle like everyone else knew I was going to get fired before I did. Afterwards I remember telling everybody the reason I got fired was politics and because I was a Christian.

One morning after this happened, I was praying and I heard God's still small voice loud and clear. He said I was to stop saying that and tell the truth. The truth was that even though I was the best at what I did, I worked for someone else and following directions meant to do it their way not my way. Thinking I knew better, I did things my way. Then when they inspected my work they found out I had done it my way not their way.

As soon as I started telling the truth about why I was fired, the door opened for me to start my own business.

So, I began telling everybody the truth was that I could've done a better job and that I hadn't followed instructions.

I guess the moral of the story is you can be the best at something and still get fired. Your pride will get you fired. Pride is one of the main things that kept me from growing up and it needed to go. Even still today that is part of my prayer. One of the good things about being a Christian is when God shuts one door another one opens up. So, I guess you could say God killed two birds with one stone, my pride and my poverty.

Our 1st All Expenses Paid Out of Town Business Trip

Our Own Business

We started our own business while we were on food stamps and Section 8. The business took off like a rocket. I worked the field and Melody worked the office. Our lives together were another example of how with God all things are possible (Mark 10:27). We became a success story about the time the movie, "Pursuit of Happyness,"[7] came out.

Our local news station contacted the SAMMinistries Homeless Shelter looking for just such a success story. At this point in our business, we were still on food stamps and living off Section 8, just a step above homelessness and just a step away from being free from government help, learning how to completely depend on God. I agreed to an interview as long as they promised to give credit where credit was due. They said sure and asked who that would be.

"Jesus, of course," I said with a great big smile across my face.

During the interview, all I could talk about was Jesus, my new found peace and joy, and all my experiences at VGC SGC. When the interview aired, they only used comments about SAMMinistries and said nothing about VGC SGC.

At the end, though, they did keep their word showing me and my family walking up the sidewalk into our Section 8, two-story, four-bedroom, two-bath house with my voice saying, "I don't have to worry about a house, a job, what I'm going to drive or anything else I need in this life. All I have to do is fall in love with Jesus and all these things shall be added unto me, quoting Matthew 6:33."

---

[7] The Pursuit of Happyness is a 2006 American biographical drama film based on Chris Gardner's nearly one-year struggle being homeless.

Within six months, we no longer needed the government's help, and today we own that house.

Start Where You Are, Use What You Have and Do What You Can

In Judges 3:31, we read the story of a man named Shamgar, the son of Anath, who slew 600 Philistine men with an ox goad and delivered Israel. The story of Shamgar is an inspiration to me because it is about a man, who against all odds, got the victory. He started where he was, he used what he had, and he did what he could. Most people would like to start over, but the reality of it is, that's impossible. What we can do is start again and use what we already have.

We need to stop waiting for the perfect circumstances, the right amount of money or more education. God is asking us, "What's in your hand?" Moses had a rod in his hand and he used it to part the Red Sea. Then he used the same rod to cause water to come from a rock and bring fire down from heaven. Miriam held the tambourine and led Israel in praise. Hannah held a child who became a great prophet. Ruth held a stock of grain that fed her family, and a little boy with a sack lunch gave it to Jesus who fed 5000 people with it.

I had to start again right where I was on food stamps and Section 8. I had a caulking gun in my hand and I did what I could. Today, we run a successful, growing business. Today, I try to make as much money as I can for the furthering of God's Kingdom. I believe if it was for any other reason I would not be so successful.

Colossians 1:16 in The Message Bible says, "For everything, abso-lutely everything, above and below, visible and invisible, everything got started in Him and finds its purpose in Him" (MSG). Ephesians 1:11 says, "In Christ we find who we are" (MSG). In Christ is how we discover ourselves. Romans 8:6 says, "Stop obsessing with self because it's a dead end and start with God, attention toward God opens doors to a free life not merely existing but truly living" (MSG). The truth is, God's way is easy, it is our way that is hard. Proverbs 14:12 says, "There is a way that seems right unto a man but in the end it leads to death."

It's not about you and what you want. It's about God and what He wants, so start where you are. Start again. Start with God. Use what you've got in your hand, the Word of God. Do what you can. Hebrews 4:12 says, "For the word of God is quick and powerful and sharper than any two edged sword." Galatians 2:20 says, "I have been crucified with Christ. I no longer live but Christ lives in me." The first thing you have is the Word of God. Start with what God says about you, not what the world says about you. Use what you've got. God's given you a gift. He has placed within you all that you need to succeed. What you are is God's gift to you. What you do with yourself is your gift to God.[8]

Ephesians 5:17 says, "Don't act thoughtlessly, but try to find out and do whatever the Lord wants you to do" (NLT). Galatians 6:4 says, "Do your own work well and then you will have something to be proud of, but don't compare yourself to others" (CEV). Start where you are. Start again with God. Use what you have in your hand. Use the Word

---

[8]   *Purpose Driven Life,* Rick Warren

of God and your God given talent. Do what you can. Put your hand to the plow, pray, and praise the God who has given you life, ability, and purpose. Do things God's way and you will find your way to your purpose and prosperity.

Ask Yourself. . .

- *Am I frustrated, disillusioned, and hard to get along with?*
- *Have I been thinking I know better, and doing things my way?*
- *Can I see now that I need to change some things in my life so I can break this pattern?*
- *Do I really want God to lead me to fulfill my purpose in life?*
- *Am I willing to do whatever it takes to truly move forward with my life?*

God looks to and fro looking to find someone to show himself strong in.
(2 Chronicles 16:9)

Poems from Prison

In and out of jail back and forth with You
Still You stuck around and endured all my abuse.

I believed there had to be a reason for such a strong obsession
For You to stick around and always offer me protection

Love and grace I knew but there had to be something else
There had to be a purpose it was something that I felt.

My flesh didn't like the feeling and I started to fear
That if it got any stronger the fog would began to clear

I was afraid to see myself for what I had become
I was headed for destruction so again I had to run

Finally in prison with 11 ½ years to serve
Still You were there with me so to You I finally turned.

- Anthony Monda

Chapter 6

God's Ways Are Higher than Our Ways

"My thoughts are nothing like your thoughts," says the LORD. *"And my ways are far beyond anything you could imagine. For just as the heavens are higher than the earth, so my ways are higher than your ways and my thoughts higher than your thoughts.* (Isaiah 55:8-9 NLT)

Knowing "The Way"

Back in high school, I was the punt return specialist on my school football team. The game was 0 to 0 in the fourth quarter. The coach told me to catch the ball this time in the air and run straight out of bounds to stop the clock. There were only a few seconds left in the game. I was the kind of punt returner who liked to catch punts on the bounce so I'm not looking up and can see the approaching opposing team. I thought my only job was to catch the ball, keep from getting tackled, and score a touchdown. I never understood **the way** the play was designed. That night, I was about to learn I was trying to score a touchdown the **hard way** by not taking advantage of **the way** the play was intended to work.

Normally during the game, I couldn't hear the fans, the coaches, and my family cheering from the sidelines, I just heard a constant roar. But that night when I let the ball bounce I could hear my coach screaming at top of his lungs, "What are you doing?" It was a line drive punt low to the ground and the other team was down the field right on top of it hovering over the ball waiting for it to roll its last turn before they downed it. I was standing on the other side of the ball with my hands on my hips, giving no clue to what I was about to do. Just at the right time, right before the ball came to a final stop, I reached down like the Flash, picked up the ball, and raced to the sideline to stop the clock.

Lo and behold, when I got there I noticed that our defensive lineman had formed a wall lined up in single file along the sideline with a clear passageway to the goal line about 60 yards away. So, I turned up field and as the clock ran down, I ran all the way for a touchdown crossing the goal line just as the buzzer went off to end the game. We won. The bench cleared and I was mauled in celebration by my teammates.

Punt Return

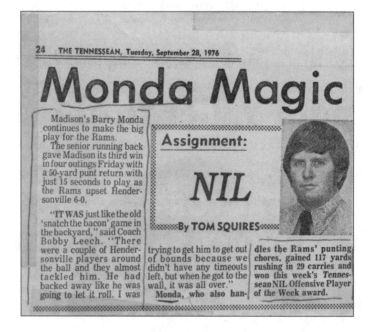

24   THE TENNESSEAN, Tuesday, September 28, 1976

Monda Magic

Madison's Barry Monda continues to make the big play for the Rams.

The senior running back gave Madison its third win in four outings Friday with a 50-yard punt return with just 15 seconds to play as the Rams upset Hendersonville 6-0.

"IT WAS just like the old 'snatch the bacon' game in the backyard," said Coach Bobby Leech. "There were a couple of Hendersonville players around the ball and they almost tackled him. He had backed away like he was going to let it roll. I was

Assignment:

NIL

By TOM SQUIRES

trying to get him to get out of bounds because we didn't have any timeouts left, but when he got to the wall, it was all over."

Monda, who also han-

dles the Rams' punting chores, gained 117 yards rushing in 29 carries and won this week's *Tennessean* NIL Offensive Player of the Week award.

Monda Magic

92

If I'd known **the way** the play was supposed to go, how many more punt return touchdowns might there have been in my playing career? As Christians, knowing **the way** of the Lord is very important. The disciples were with Jesus for three years 24/7. They sat under His teachings day and night. Yet in the end, they forsook Him and fled because they did not know His **ways**.

The seventy elders of Israel ate and drank in God's very presence on the Mount, yet the Lord said to them, "You never got to know Me or **My ways**." In Matthew 22:29 Jesus said, "You do err not knowing the Scriptures nor the power of God." To err means to stray, to wander, to be out of **the way**. In John 14:6 Jesus said, "I am **the way**, the truth, and the life."

As Christians, when we go through our unpleasant life experiences, we tend to wander off in the wrong direction on our own and try to do things **our way**. **God's way** is to take us through these stormy times and bring us out stronger on the other side of them.

When Jesus came walking on the water during the storm, the disciples were afraid. They did not recognize Jesus because they did not know **His ways**. He said, "Be not afraid, it is I." In other words, He was telling them, "I allowed that situation and that circumstance. I allowed that storm of correction, that storm of perfection, but be not afraid, it is I." Though we are going through situations, circumstances, storms of correction, storms of perfection, and wilderness experiences, Jesus is with us. God uses storms to get us to our knees so we will learn to seek to do things **His way**. He said He would never leave or forsake us no matter what it seems like we are facing in our lives.

We just need to get on our knees, trust Him to make us free of fear, and take us to the next level of our journey, **His way**. If we never have a wilderness experience, we will never experience God's faithfulness. If we never go through a storm, we will never know that God can bring us safely through it.

If we never have any problems, we will never know God can and will solve them, His way.

> *For You, O God, have tested us;*
> *You have refined us as silver is refined.*
> *You brought us into the net;*
> *You laid affliction on our backs.*
> *You have caused men to ride over our heads;*
> **We went through fire and through water;**
> **But You brought us out to rich fulfillment.** (or wealthy place in KJV).
> (Psalm 66:10 NKJV emphasis added)

So next time you go through something, don't come up missing. Go to your knees and let God bring you out into a wealthy place. Psalm 34:19 says, "Many are the afflictions of the righteous but God delivers us from them all." Storms, wilderness experiences, and affliction are all designed to pull you into God's presence and into a wealthy place. 1 Corinthians 10:13 says, "No temptation has overtaken you except such as is common to man; but God is faithful, who will not allow you to be tempted beyond what you are able, but with the temptation will also make the way of escape, that you may be able to bear it."

God's way doesn't always feel good. Dr. Bishop Donny Banks' preaching from behind the pulpit pulled me up and out of sin. He then got behind me with the "taught" Word and pushed me out of my comfort zone into God's plan for my life.

> **Escape to your knees in prayer and come out into a wealthy place God's way.**

If I had never let God use the man of God to push me out of my comfort zone and teach me **God's ways**, I would never have known God like I know Him today. I would never have become a man of God, and a godly husband, father, homeowner, business owner, elder, pastor, and published author of a best seller that points to Jesus. None of this would have come to pass without stepping out in faith and believing **with God all things are possible!**

The preached Word will get you saved and the taught Word will keep you saved. Always stay teachable.

God wants us to exercise our faith and to grow in the knowledge of how He wants things done. He has promised to give us everything we need for a life of godliness through our knowledge of Him who called us into His service. Through His great and precious promises,

He has given us everything we need to escape the corruption of the world and achieve success (2 Peter 1:3-4). However, we need to do our part and become skilled and use the tools He has given us.

Blind Faith Swing Batter, Swing!

The new kid was the talk of the town. He was from California, so he automatically became a giant in our eyes. He was the number one "grade A" pitcher who came relentlessly with a side-arm fastball to strike everyone out. Because of my speed and the ability to steal bases, I was the first in the batting order. I played third base and hardly anything got passed me. When it came to batting I had the good stance, a good swing, eye to the ball contact, but no bat to ball contact because I had no confidence. Before the first pitch I already felt humiliated. When the first pitch came, I froze like a statue. The ball came right down the middle, a perfect pitch. Strike one. My mind was racing. I couldn't let this guy from California strike me out. The second pitch came, again right down the middle, strike two.

I thought to myself, if I was going out I was going out swinging. So, I got in my good stance and cocked my bat back for a good hard swing. I watched the ball as it left the pitcher's hand and believe it or not, I closed my eyes and swung the bat as hard as I could. The top of the bat made contact with the bottom of the ball which launched it like a rocket high into the sky, but I didn't know where it went. The crowd cheered as I ran as fast as I could to first base and was headed to second when I saw the ball barely drop over the centerfield fence. I was twelve years old and that was my first and last home run hit I had in my life.

Swing Batter!

The moral of the story is, it's time to step up to the plate of life and don't be afraid to swing the bat. Go for the homerun. Dream big. Never stop dreaming. Never stop swinging. Don't just dream—swing. Just ask my teammate and best bud from across the street who went on to hit 3 homeruns and 2 grandslams that season.

Swing Batter! Tracy, left. Barry, right.

If you don't pray you won't stay. If you don't fast you won't last.

In Matthew 7:7-8 Jesus says, "Ask and it shall be given you, seek and you shall find, knock and it shall be opened unto you, for everyone that asks receives and he that seeks finds. Unto him that knocks, it shall be open."

In this passage, the Lord presents three realms of prayer: asking, seeking, and knocking. The physical realm is the realm of asking. The soul realm is the realm of seeking. The spiritual realm is the realm of knocking. The physical realm represents the flesh. When the flesh is still in control, it is easy to get distracted, tired, and worn out. You cannot hear God's voice there, so it gets easy to give up.

Only when we overcome the flesh can we get to the second realm, the soul realm which is the realm of seeking. Here in the realm of seeking, the Holy Spirit grants us the power to seek the Lord. Jeremiah 29:13 says, "You shall seek me and find me when you shall search for me with all your heart." Seeking God will cause your heart to be filled with His Word.

The spirit realm, the realm of knocking is the Holy of Holies. This realm represents God's presence. God speaks to us when we enter into the Holy of Holies. The spiritual realm is the deepest form of intimacy with the Lord. There are no shortcuts. You have to go through the process. You have to go through the three realms of prayer to get into the Holy of Holies and hear God. When I pray, I don't always get into the Holy of Holies. Usually it's because I'm distracted with the cares of this world or my prayers have become more of a routine than from my heart.[9]

Once a month our teen ministry goes somewhere fun to give the teens memories, good memories, of God and church. One Tuesday we went to see the movie, "Everest." Reminded me in a lot of ways about my prayer life and how every morning prayer was like climbing Mt Everest to get into God's presence and it was no easy task. In the beginning as a baby Christian God's presence and revelations come easy but after a while it's like "hide and seek." We have to learn how to

[9]   Benny Hinn, *Three Realms of Prayer*

hunt through prayer and searching the scriptures to find His presence and to receive deeper understanding of His Word.

In the *Purpose Driven Life*, Rick Warren tells us the most common mistake Christians make in worship today is seeking an experience rather than seeking God. They look for a feeling, and if it happens, they conclude that they have worshiped. Seeking a feeling, even the feeling of closeness to Christ, is not worship. When you are baby Christian, God gives you a lot of confirming emotions and often answers the most immature, self-centered prayers so you will know He exists.

However, as you grow, He will wean you of these dependencies.

Fasting and Prayer—Tools for Achieving Success

The Key to Effective Prayer

(Taken from a Sermon by Derek Prince)

This biblical key will cause a breakthrough in your prayer life. Failure to use this biblical key causes my life as a Christian to be ineffective in the body of Christ. Matthew 6:5-6 clearly tells us how not to pray and how to pray. The Bible says when you pray, do not pray like the hypocrites.

The Bible expresses there is a negative way to pray and a positive way to pray. Also in Matthew 6:16-17 it says when you fast, do not fast like the hypocrites.

In this passage it also tells us that there is a positive and a negative way to fast. These two scriptures start with "when you pray. . . when you fast" not if you pray or if you fast.

John Wesley says, "I am persuaded that if a Christian understands the need to fast and doesn't, they will backslide just like if you don't pray."

You may ask yourself what's the purpose of fasting? To make my life hard or to deny me pleasure? No, it is God's appointed way for us to humble ourselves.

Our barrier to answered prayer is pride. Pride gets us all. We need to get pride out of the way and get our prayers answered. Our perfect example is the first sin.

Pride caused an angel (Lucifer) to lose his place. How much more can we as Christians lose our place because of pride? Don't think it can't happen to you. The Bible says when you think you stand be careful lest you fall (1 Corinthians 10:12).

God tells us to humble ourselves (Luke 14:11). He never says that He will humble us, but God will allow humiliation so we will humble ourselves so He can honor us (James 4:10). God will do the lifting up but we have to humble ourselves.

There was a man who heard a sermon about fasting and decided to fast the next day. All day long as he walked by the fast food restaurants, looking through the glass window of the bakery, and smelling the freshly made doughnuts, he came to the conclusion that it had been a terrible day. So he said to his stomach, "Stomach you caused me a lot of discomfort today so I'm going to punish you." I'm going to fast again tomorrow. Your stomach is a wonderful servant but a terrible master.

James 42:3 The Bible says, "You have not because you ask not and when you do ask you ask amiss." In other words, you asked with the wrong motives. I would like to add that if fasting is not part of your asking, you pray amiss. Jesus said some things only come out by prayer and fasting. Through prayer and fasting, Esther and Nehemiah both found favor with the king.

In Proverbs 21:1 it says God holds the heart of the King in His hand. God also holds the heart of your spouse, your boss, the IRS, and all the judges and juries in His hand. God holds the heart of every situation, circumstance, and endeavor in His hands, too.

Has your prayer life seemed to become just another habit? Fast and pray. Having trouble praying from the heart? Fast and pray. Do you find yourself always praying amiss? Fast and pray. Haters seem like they've got the upper hand? Fast and pray.

When I was in the Spiritual Growth Center, I started my fast by going last in line during meal time and memorizing scripture as I slowly moved forward in line. You know the Bible does say the last shall be first and the first shall be last (Matthew 20:16). Then at night we would have snack time and I would fast snack time and read my Bible. Then I graduated to breakfast. Slowly but surely I fasted lunch then dinner and eventually fasted all day and just drank water which gave me more time with the Lord. The only way to get to know somebody better is to spend more time them.

F stands for **F**eed the spirit and not the flesh.

A stands for **A**doration and **A**ttention, a deep love and respect toward God and giving God more of your attention.

S stands for **S**erve and **S**ecret, make it a point to serve and keep your fast between you and God.

T stands for the **T**ruth, because if you know the truth about fasting the Truth will make you free.

➤ Fasting and prayer demonstrate repentance.

➤ Fasting and prayer are ways to appeal to God for forgiveness and pardon.

➤ Fasting and prayer give you God's protection, provision, and productivity.

➤ Fasting and prayer resolves tension in relationships.

➤ Fasting and prayer keeps you from oppressing others.

➤ Fasting and prayer draws you closer to God.

➤ Fasting and prayer intensifies worship.

➤ Fasting and prayer brings spiritual blessing and insight.

➤ Fasting and prayer brings divine rewards and divine revelation.

➤ Fasting and prayer should be incorporated into your life on a regular basis to help bring your flesh under submission.

➤ Fasting and prayer helps you become more sensitive to the moving of the Holy Spirit.

Ask Yourself. . .

- *Am I willing to humble myself and fast and pray so I can mature and grow into the person God has designed me to be?*

- *Am I willing to let God move me out of my comfort zone so He can use me to be a productive member of His kingdom business?*

- *What is God telling me I need to do to achieve this and weather my current storm?*

2007 Family Photo Our visit with Anthony in Juvie -

Left to right in back: Melody, Barry, and Anthony.

Front: Catheryn and Jared.

Poems from Prison

The beginning was kind of empty our relationship started slow
I wanted all Your blessings but still didn't want to grow.

I constantly hurt myself always trying to manipulate
Always abusing Your grace playing with reprobate.

My prayer life increased slowly my mind renewed
I made up my mind of the choice I was going to chose.

I started forgiving my family I knew they weren't to blame
I recognized that I was sick inside and on myself I brought the pain.

Forgiving myself was harder thinking of the hurt I caused
But through You I endured and started to grow strong.

Praying without ceasing meditating on Your word
It came to me suddenly You put me here to serve

Still a baby Christian learning how to walk
Recognize that with Your help in you I'll never fall.

But if I do and trials and storms come my way
I'll be like my father put my trust in You
And on the Rock, my Foundation will stay.

- Anthony Monda

Chapter 7

It Pays to Obey

Early on in the business, I can remember being super busy. One day I received a call from a sign company that wanted me to do some night work at the mall. I told him that I was too busy and didn't have the time, but still they pressed me for a price and would not take no for an answer. So, I tripled my price thinking this would get rid of them. To my surprise they answered my proposal with a phone call asking me when I could start. Looks like I'm working nights! Part of the deal was that they would supply all materials. So toward the end of the job, I asked their superintendent if I could have a couple of cases of the leftover caulk for another job that was coming up.

Fasting is the key to answered prayer and to walking in the spirit and not the flesh.

He said "Sure, you can have as much as you want, just don't tell anybody."

Everything would've been fine if he had not said those four words. I decided to finish up the job and get out of there. I wasn't about to jeopardize all the good that God was doing in my life by stealing, but for some reason this guy, the superintendent, would not leave me alone about getting that material. Before I could get away, he caught up with me and asked me to follow him in my truck to the parking garage.

I followed him around the mall making my way to the parking garage where the material was. While on the way, I asked God to help me to do what I needed to do in a way that wouldn't belittle the supervisor.

As we pulled up to the spot, we both get out of our vehicles and he immediately brought the cases over to me.

As he turned his back and walked away I said, "Hey, before I put these in my truck there is something I need to say."

It was the end of the night and everybody was headed home. The supervisor and about five guys were cleaning up and putting away their tools. I began to explain how a couple years back I gave my life to Jesus and accepted Him as my personal Lord and Savior and that He had blessed me with my own business and I didn't want to do anything to mess that up. That's when God showed up. I had everybody's attention. Frustrated, I began telling everyone that I didn't even want the job. I was too busy and the people they worked for paid me triple what I normally make. I told them I thought that was why I was on the job. but God has just shown me that it was not about the job and it was not about the money, it was about right here, right now.

"There is somebody here that God is after and you know who you are." There was a young man who had stayed busy in the background while everyone else stopped and listened, but as soon as I said those words our eyes met. I believe it was him who God was calling and God had me deliver that personal message to him that day. I felt God's presence strong that night. He answered my prayer and He gave me what to say.

Every time I tell the story someone always asks me, "Did you take the material?" Yes, I did, and when I got back to the office, I sat down and wrote out a check for the two cases with a thank you note to those who had given me the job and the extra material.

It pays to obey.

Follow Instructions

Some lessons I learned the hard way. For example, I took on work I should not have taken on and made several mistakes that almost cost me everything. My wife had been telling me to take advantage of the opportunity to hear Dave Ramsey whenever he was in town giving seminars. She also advised me to read his books about starting and running our own business. She actually ordered two of his books, but I had just left them sitting on my desk collecting dust. Business was good. Life was good and I was comfortable with the way God had been blessing me already. I finally read one of the books, *Financial Peace*. It was about how to budget and make your money work for you.

The other book, *EntreLeadership*, was about how to start and run a business which I felt I had already done.

Though I enjoyed the first book, I didn't think I needed the other one since things were going so good. About that time, I began to make lots of mistakes and was struggling to stay in business. It got so bad, my wife resigned from the business that we had started together. The tension between us was so heavy we separated and I moved out.

Desperately seeking God for a quick fix, I finally obeyed God and picked up the book by Dave Ramsey and began reading it. That very day a weight was lifted and things begin to change. As I read the book, every mistake I had made was there in black and white. I began to realize that God had given me the book via my wife to keep me from making all those mistakes and to grow the business instead of go out of business.

It reminded me of the times I would run to the park and back taking my two dogs (Labrador retrievers) with me. They were so used to me running to the park and back along the same path, they would run ahead of me and would be playing in the pond when I got there. One day I decided to go a different way and turned down an unfamiliar street. The dogs started out toward the park, but then came running back and stayed right beside me because they've never been that way before.

God showed me that I was so used to being blessed the same way, running the business the same way, and doing things the same way that when God took a right toward growth and prosperity, I ran to the park! Does that make my dogs smarter than me? In doing so I had missed the training God was offering me through someone with more experience and knowledge.

My wife once told me about a dream she had about walking with God on a path where everything was beautiful. It was full of bright colors and overwhelming aromas that came from a mixture of flowers. As they were walking down the path hand-in-hand, every time something pretty caught Melody's eye she would let go of God's hand, leave the path, and run over to it to get a closer look. However, God never left the path and always waited for Melody to come back and then they would continue down the path.

So it is with life. We're on our life's journey and in God's perfect will. We can get distracted by the things of the world and when we do, they slow us down prolonging our arrival to where God is trying to take us to another place in Him. Everything in God is always moving forward to a higher plain. It's never stagnant. Everything in God always grows, whether it **It pays to obey.** is spiritually or naturally.

Obedience Is Better than Sacrifice

But Samuel replied, "What is more pleasing to the LORD: your burnt offerings and sacrifices or your obedience to his voice? Listen! Obedience is better than sacrifice, and submission is better than offering the fat of rams." (1 Samuel 15:22 NLT)

God tells us in His Word that obedience is better than sacrifice. He also says in Isaiah 1:19 if we are willing and obedient we shall eat of the good of the land. 2 Chronicles 20:20 is what I call the perfect vision verse, "Believe in the Lord your God, and you shall be established; believe His prophets, and you shall prosper" (NKJV).

A company owed us lots of money and had for almost a year and they were asking us to do more work for them. It was good business sense that my office refuse the job. However, in my heart of hearts I felt God said go and do the work. My directions were not very good and being sometimes directionally challenged, I just couldn't find the place. I got lost and came across a new CVS that was under construction. I stopped to express my availability to do work for them and left them one of my business cards. When I finally arrived at the job I couldn't find, I was greeted with a big fat check. I also was awarded the CVS contract.

After the work was done for the company that had owed us all the money, I shared a meal with the owner. He talked the whole time about all that had been going on in his business and his personal life. I just listened. When we finished eating, he prayed for both of us. Later, he called saying how much he enjoyed our time together and that we should do it more often. He said he really appreciated me listening.

Listening is very important during our prayer time with the Lord as well. I know when I pray I usually find myself doing all the talking. I forget sometimes that God created the whole world and everything in it so He is all knowing. He is the source of everything we need and

112

yet we think we need to do all the talking. So next time when you're finished praying, pause for a few minutes and listen. God wants to talk to you. It pays to listen and it pays to obey.

Listen and Obey

Early on in business, a caulking company down in the Valley ran out of money and couldn't finish the job, so we were called in to take over, with a guaranteed profit.

Visiting the job site, I dropped by the local supply house and ran into the guy I was replacing. On my way home God spoke to me in His still small voice that I'd grown used to hearing and usually brought tears to my eyes. God wanted me to offer my help to this guy financially and every other way. I thought to myself that this just doesn't make any sense. However, in obedience and defying all logic, I reached for my phone. Just as I did, I was over shadowed by what I believed to have been a Texas size kamikaze vulture crashing into the windshield of my vehicle aiming for my head. Was it coincidence or was it the devil? To me it was conformation and I made the call!

When I called him and explained how I believed God wanted me to help him finish the job, he said, "I know God, too. I don't want your help. I don't need your help. Down here in the Valley we stick together, we help each other."

It pays to be obedient to God!

He hung up. It was like he didn't hear a word I said. Again I realized it was not about the job and it was not about the money. It was about being obedient to God. Needless to say, we ended up taking the job over and it was one of our biggest jobs with one of our highest profits.

Ask Yourself. . .

- *Have I ever been tempted to compromise my standards for what I thought was for the greater good?*
- *How did that work out for me?*
- *Do I now see that obedience to God is better than sacrifice?*
- *Is there an area of disobedience I need to deal with in my life?*

Conclusion

It's Never Too Late

G od has placed a desire in my heart to share my story. I was a drug addict who lived a backslidden life for many years. While I was away from God, He wasn't away from me. My life is proof that God can truly redeem and restore lives and I want others to know He can do that for them, too.

I was in my mess so long that everyone gave up on me, but God never gave up on me. Some of us have loved ones or know someone with life-controlling problems that are looking for a way out. Using my life experiences in my addiction and how Christ has redeemed me will give hope to you and your loved ones that it's never too late. No matter how low you or your loved one has hit, God is faithful and just to forgive you of all unrighteousness and will meet you right where you are. God can and will pick you up and start you on the journey to restoration and redemption. His desire is to empower you to live a successful life in Him. So let go and let God do what only He can do.

K.I.S.S. Keep It Simple Saint! Living the Christian life is not as hard as you think. It is as simple as 1, 2, 3.

1-**Go**

2-**Grow**

3-**Know**

So let us stop going over the basic teachings about Christ again and again. Let us go on instead and become mature (grow) *in our understanding* (know). (Hebrews 6:1 NLT emphasis added)

1) GO to church.

2) GROW and mature by faith through the hearing of the Word of God.

3) KNOW Him and the power of His resurrection. Because He got up, you can get up.

Ephesians 2:3 says salvation is a free gift of God. Won't you accept that free gift today?

The Bible says today is the day of salvation. Now is the time. Repeat this prayer with me:

Father, in the name of Jesus, please forgive me all of my sins. Come into my heart. Change my heart. Come into my mind. Change my mind. Come into my life. Change my life. Jesus, I accept You as my personal Lord and Savior and whatever You do don't let me miss heaven. In the name of the Father, the Son, and the Holy Spirit. Amen.

The Bible says in Romans 10:9, "That if you confess with your mouth the Lord Jesus and believe in your heart that God has raised Him from the dead, you will be saved."

Congratulations on a new life in Him! Now find a good church that preaches and teaches the written Word of God. Not just a feel-good message but the truth and nothing but the truth. There is a God. There is a devil. There is a heaven. There is a hell. Today you have a choice to make. "But as for me and my house, we will serve the Lord" (Joshua 24:15).

Promotion Left to right: Prophetess Jackie Banks, Elder Barry,

Bishop Donny Banks.

About the Author

Barry Monda is a youth pastor, elder, successful business owner, and now a published author. He grew up in a middle-class family. He excelled in sports from the time he was eight years old until he flunked out in his second year in college where he lost a full football scholarship at Austin Peay State University. At the age of nineteen, he got a job working construction and continued a downhill spiral. By the time he was twenty-three, he was smoking crack, in and out of rehabs, spiritual growth centers, half-way houses, and jail for the next two decades. At the age of forty-four, a miraculous transformation took place in his life and today he has been standing strong for twelve years. He now gives hope to others struggling with addiction.

**Contact the
author at: barrysmonda@gmail.com**